THE LANGUAGE OF ORDINARY EXPERIENCE

A Study in the Philosophy of Education

by

David E. Denton

University of Kentucky

Philosophical Library

New York

Copyright, 1970, by PHILOSOPHICAL LIBRARY, INC.
15 East 40th Street, New York, New York 10016
All rights reserved
Library of Congress Catalog Card No. 72-100580
SBN 8022-2312-5
MANUFACTURED IN THE UNITED STATES OF AMERICA

"Art, at least, teaches us that man cannot be explained by history alone."

—Camus in *The Rebel*

PREFACE

This study divides readily into three parts, parts which, though easily identifiable as a result of the different focus of each, cannot be understood apart. This is to say that, although the book is divided into parts and chapters, it is actually a multi-dimensional whole, tapestry rather than taxonomy. All parts, chapters, and sections, thus, are to be interpreted accordingly.

Part One consists of four chapters which, together, provide the grounds for the assertion that education is first-person experience and set forth the language and conceptual tools needed for talking of education from that perspective. Chapter I locates the key concepts of the work in the stream of Western thought; Chapter II summarizes and criticizes most of the philosophy of language work which has been done in education; Chapter III refines the definition of the term *ordinary experience;* and Chapter IV develops the language tools for talking of ordinary experience.

Taken together, the first four chapters consist of arguments against sociological-nomothetic approaches to the study of education, with the primary attack being directed toward attempts to talk of education with steno-language, and of arguments for a radically different conception of education, one which is grounded in the ordinary experience of individuals, with ways quite different from steno-language being proposed for talking of education.

Part Two consists of Chapters V and VI, which focus on two specific topics in the philosophy of education, with the tools of criticism and analysis being the concepts and arguments developed in the first four chapters. Chapter V treats of the question of knowledge, and Chapter VI, that of explanation. To delimit these very broad topics to manageable sizes and to make them most relevant to the purposes of this work, the chapter on knowledge focuses on that problem in its relation to curriculum and teaching, while the chapter on explanation is focused on the explanation of human action as that is attempted in counseling.

In Part Three the direction of the weave of the fabric changes once again, this time to a relating of the work to this point against the backdrop of the larger tapestry of existential philosophy and to a projection regarding certain additional outcomes of the extension of the fabric of this work. More specifically, the first of the remaining two chapters treats of the relationships between existential language and existential philosophy, pointing up the affinity for, but the difference from, one and the other. In a sense, then, this last section moves to topics larger in scope than those two specialized ones of the preceding section. The last chapter does not summarize what has been said in the first seven, but, rather, concludes by suggesting the possible bearings of the first seven chapters on two additional matters, organizational theory and a specific, current social issue.

ACKNOWLEDGMENTS

Appreciation is expressed to the following publishers for permission to quote from the works indicated:
—McGraw-Hill Book Co. G. Schrader, *Existential Philosophers: Kierkegaard to Merleau-Ponty,* 1967.
—Saturday Review, Inc. J. Culkin, "A Schoolman's Guide to Marshall McLuhan," March 18, 1967.
—John Wiley & Sons, Inc. C. Hall and G. Lindzey, *Theories of Personality,* 1957.
—Pantheon Books. A. Watts, *The Book,* 1966.
—Wesleyan University Press. N. Brown, *Life Against Death,* 1959.
—Indiana University Press. P. Wheelwright, *Metaphor and Reality,* 1962.
—Libra Publishers, Inc. P. Koestenbaum, "Phenomenological Foundations of the Behavioral Sciences: The Nature of Facts," *The Journal of Existentialism,* Spring 1966.
—Alfred A. Knopf, Inc. A. Camus, *The Myth of Sisyphus and Other Essays,* 1959.
And thanks must be extended to certain individuals and groups who have provided critical assistance at significant points in the development of the work:
—Professor Stephen Mooney, The University of Tennessee, whose work in the philosophy and poetics of language has stimulated my own;
—Professor Philip Wheelwright, University of California, and Professor Peter Koestenbaum, San Jose State College, whose thought, expressed in their writings and in correspondence, assisted in the clarification of certain concepts basic to the chapter on existential language;
—Professor Raymond Wilkie, University of Kentucky, who gave very careful attention to the chapter on explanation;

—members of the Philosophy of Education Society who have reacted in a variety of helpful ways to the ideas of this work as these have been presented in their formative statements in papers and articles;

—students who have been willing to explore the possibilities of a language for speaking of their own individual experience and whose contributions of examples and illustrations appear throughout the work;

—finally, Shari, wife and soul-mate, whose ordinary experience she communicates quite well without the aid of any book.

But stimulation, assistance, careful attention, reactions, and explorations—all from others—do not constitute the grounds for responsibility; that is mine alone.

David E. Denton
Lexington, Kentucky
1969

CONTENTS

THE LANGUAGE OF ORDINARY EXPERIENCE

PART ONE

Chapter I

FROM SOCIOLOGY TO ORDINARY EXPERIENCE

The Existential Paradox

The existential paradox may be expressed by the mutual exclusiveness of the following two sentences:
A. My life has no significance, no meaning, to the ongoingness of the universe.
B. My life is the center of the universe.
The truth of sentence A comes to us in our recognition that during our life-spans we control little of that which is called nature and society and that, following our deaths, even less of that which we did remains in any form. Even the largest waves in the ocean of time leave little, if any, effect on that ocean. The span of man's life is short enough, but, when placed in the perspective of historical time, that span is infinitesimal. Yet, in those moments when the truth of sentence A overwhelms us, another truth, that of sentence B, persistently knocks at the door of awareness. For when the world is looked at from the phenomenological perspective of the individual, the truth of sentence B becomes apparent. I am at the center of the universe; anything I ever say about the world will be from my perspective; universal perspectives are impossible, and universal statements are true in an exact inverse proportion to their dehumanizing me.
But it is much easier to speak of sentences of type A than those of type B. Western man has become quite expert in developing the language and conceptual tools needed for carrying on discourse of type A, while sentences of type B have been attended to only by some mystics and certain poets. The language tools for dealing with sentences of type B are still at a very primitive level of development, so much so that they have been ignored by the majority of Western philosophers. To be more exact, the language tools for deal-

ing with sentences of type B have been ignored by the mainstream of Western intellectual history. We have been much more concerned with universal ideas, or grand designs of history, or universal moral codes, or scientific verification, or formalized language systems to attend very much to the idiographic, gestalt, protean nature of sentences of type B.

Education, very much a part of this Western intellectual tradition, has attempted to define itself, organize itself, justify itself, and construct theories about various aspects of itself with sentences of type A. From Plato to Bruner this has been the case. The assumption consistently held has been that laws, principles, theories could be "found" which would guide the practice of education and explain matters within, and deviancies from, that domain—thus, the resultant systems of educational organization, of curriculum, of grading, of teaching. All of these have developed from premises having sentences of type A. Suppose we consider education solely in terms of sentences of type B? Would it make a major difference in organization, curriculum, etc.? A prior matter to consider, however, before answering the question, has to do with the adequacy of our language tools for dealing with such sentences. This work attempts to grapple with two problems posed to this point: 1) to provide grounds for the claim that education must be defined in terms of sentences of type B, and 2) to set forth the language tools necessary for talking about education, and about larger social issues, from the radical perspective of the individual.

To speak more personally, this book has grown out of the writer's concern about that point of extreme tension between education's increasing complexity, on the one hand, and the increasing dissatisfaction, disenchantment, even alienation of students and faculties, on the other. From this concern a criticism has developed, namely, that most of the linguistic and conceptual tools with which education has been studied and analyzed are totally inadequate and should be scrapped by the wayside of history, and, furthermore, that the linguistic and conceptual tools referred to have been the result of a seriously mistaken conception of the nature of education. From this criticism has developed a thesis, namely, that education is ultimately a first-person

4

experience, and that, even though the philosophic problems entailed in talking of education this way are many, new and adequate linguistic and conceptual tools can be provided. Obviously, if one begins at a different starting point for his inquiry and uses different language-tools, the conclusions, ramifications, consequences will be at considerable variance from the conventional. This work, however, does not attempt to explore all such conclusions, ramifications, and consequences; it does not, therefore, attempt to be a comprehensive book on the philosophy of education, or on educational methodology, or on educational research. What it does attempt is the clarification of the social and philosophic grounds for the new starting point of inquiry and the setting forth of the language-tools required by this perspective.

Although the work is not the "philosophy of somebody," the very nature of the criticisms and of the thesis indicates something of the writer's philosophic bias. It is sufficient, at this point, to say that the author's thinking is much more in the tradition of Bergson, James, Heidegger, Sartre, Camus, and Merleau-Ponty than that of Russell, Peirce, Ayer, and Wittgenstein. Among contemporaries, I find the thought of Wheelwright and McLuhan much more exciting and suggestive for philosophy of education than the work, say, of Peters and Scheffler.[1]

All of this is not to indicate a doctrinaire commitment, but is to communicate the general tone and orientation of the book. Now that I have put my philosophic cards on the table, let the work begin.

Conventionally Speaking

Conventionally, inquiry into the nature of education has begun with some conception of society, or of knowledge, or of mind, or of man. Typical questions of those who have started with society are "What is the nature of the school as an institution?" "What is the nature of social learning?" "What are the roles of teachers, students, and administrators?" "What purposes does a given society seek to achieve by the establishment and maintenance of educational institutions?" Of those who have begun with the problem of knowledge, typical questions are "What are the essential structures of knowledge?" "What is the relationship between structures of knowledge and the design of a curriculum?" "When can one say that a student knows a certain subject matter?" Typical questions of those who have approached education from the problem of mind are "Are the metaphors used in talking about mind appropriate for educational discourse?" "What is the relationship between different conceptions of mind and different teaching methods?" "Are directives for educational practice implied in statements regarding the nature of mind?" And, of those who have begun their inquiry into education at the question of man, typical questions are: "Is there a model of man—philosophical, theological, sociological, psychological—which will provide direction in the development of educational aims?" "What kind of man does a given society wish the schools to produce? a socially adjusted man? a thinking man? an Edwardian gentleman?"

For all that has been written both about and as a result of these conventional approaches, concerns with the topics mentioned have had major impact only at the point of educational aims, objectives, purposes. And these aims, objectives, purposes have rarely been either of adequate conceptual clarity or of a logical form which would allow derivations of guides to actual practice. A result has been that, for all the concern with the questions mentioned, educational research and practice has, in the main, gone its own way, greatly affected by its own unanalyzed assumptions but little affected by work done on the nature of educational aims. Has this state of affairs been the result of a breakdown in communication? of a lack of appreciation for the work of each other? Perhaps some of both has been involved. But it is the contention of this writer, a contention which will be dealt with later in detail, that the major responsibility lies on the shoulders of philosophers of education, for little of their work has been relevant and helpful to educational researchers, teachers, or students.

Operating, then, in what they see as being something of a philosophic vacuum, though such is impossible, educational researchers and teachers have made of primary concern "getting at the facts," "doing," and "the practical." They have not really been operating without philosophy; rather, they have been operating as pragmatists and positivists

6

without being very good at either. What has been emphasized, in such an atmosphere, has been method—method of research, method of teaching—gloriously disguised under the heading *scientific*. Given the impetus of the thought of Herbart, the learning laws of Thorndike, the statistical techniques of Pearson, the measurement devices of Binét and Otis, the behaviorism of Watson, the sociological determination of objectives of Snedden, the science of education movement was well under way by the 1920's. And given the additional impetus of the positivism of Anglo-American philosophy and sociology along with the work of Skinner in operant conditioning, with its empty organism postulate and its programmed instruction outcome, the conception of education as a science is a continuing phenomenon. A recent work, *The Technology of Teaching*,[2] not only treats of educational techniques and media, as might be supposed from the title, but attempts to cover all the topics usually thought necessary for a complete theory of education. The science of education seems to have run its positivistic course, having not only eliminated philosophy but having now reduced theory to technology.

The inquiries into education discussed to this point can now be organized into two classes. Those called the conventional approaches—those involved with the questions of society, knowledge, mind, and man—are primarily rational approaches, rational in that each begins with a conception of a category of some type and attempts to derive, from categorical statements, guides for educational practice. The other class of inquiries was referred to as positivistic, pragmatic, scientific, technological. This class is basically empirical in the sense that the concern is with originating inquiry in the domain of actual behavior. Both of these approaches, however, begin with units of investigation other than the phenomenology of individual persons involved in the educative process. Even the empiricist begins with such concepts as roles, statistical units, sets, and networks of relationhips. To illustrate from both approaches, what I have called the rationalist might set up a particular model of man and then come to the individual teacher or student, using that particular model as his goal. Or, on the basis of his theological model of man, he may look for certain characteristics in his students which are set forth in the model.

7

What I have called the empiricist may approach the individual teacher or student, not in an attempt to investigate the phenomenological world of that person, but to assign a number, or to put in an experimental class, or to study overt behavior to determine if that behavior meets the expectations of a certain role.

For the reason that both the conventional, or rational, and the scientific, or empirical, approaches begin at some point other than that of the individual person, they can be further grouped into one and referred to with the term sociology. Why the term sociology? Because, as the term was employed by Durkheim, it was intended to include both rational and empirical approaches to the description and explanation of human action. Durkheim was attempting a theory of knowledge of man which was comprehensive while at the same time logically coherent, that is, without internal contradictions. For his sociology he claimed to have achieved just that.

> It [his sociology of knowledge] keeps all the essential principles of the apriorists; but at the same time it is inspired by that positive spirit which the empiricists have striven to satisfy. It leaves the reason its specific power, but it accounts for it and does so without leaving the world of observable phenomena.[3]

Hence, with an appropriate bow to Durkheim, and with perhaps a small one to Comte, the term *sociology* will be used to include all approaches to the study of education which begin at some point other than Husserl's *Welterfahrendesleben*, that is, the individual's life-experiencing-the-world.

But, just what is this life-experiencing-the-world? Is this book an attempt to "apply" Husserl's terminology to education? to explain education in terms of the language of phenomenology? Not at all. It is an attempt to provide the language-tools for talking about education from the radical perspective of the individual as he experiences his education, an education which no one else can experience. To paraphrase Cohen:[4] the subject matter of education is distinctively human; it is not merely the lining of physiology, the application of psychological theories, an example of

8

role-theory in action, or the domain of the technician. Our starting point must be the phenomena of experience from the "inside." The paraphrase of Cohen, obviously, raises more questions than it answers, but it does point to, communicate the direction of, the inquiry of this work. If education is the phenomenon of experience from the "inside," if education is ultimately a first-person experience, how, then, can we talk meaningfully about it? That, put into different terms, is the problem which the work investigates.

From Sociology to Phenomenology

The task of sociology, for Durkheim, was to explain the nature of modern man; this he did, not by demonstrating the relation of the individual to the larger patterns of social interaction, but by asserting that the individual derived his reality from the society. He held that the social realm was one with the natural realm and that just as there were laws of nature so there were social laws.[5] Social laws, then, were not of a special order, but were simply a type of natural law, possessing all the logical powers claimed for natural laws. It would then follow that whatever definition was given for man would be one that was derived from social laws. In effect, the individual perspective is never a starting point of inquiry but is, at best, merely a particularization of some previously asserted law. In Durkheim's later years he did recognize this matter to be a problem, but, as Tiryakian has stated, Durkheim remained the foremost exponent for the movement of *solidarisme*.[6]

Very few present-day sociologists or educationists would accept Durkheim's reality claims for social laws, and yet, they are at one with him and with the dominant philosophic tradition of the West in holding that individuals are particularizations of general laws. Put in other terms, sociology agrees with Western philosophy in starting its inquiry at some category other than that of the individual and then working back to the individual. Knowledge, according to this tradition, is always prior to the individual, including knowledge of individuals. To illustrate from philosophy, a typical question would be, What is good human conduct? Answers, in the form of principles, will be established, and the necessary social machinery will be put into operation

9

(i.e., laws passed, etc.) to see that individuals comport themselves in a manner consistent with the principles of good conduct. To illustrate from sociology, a Sutherland-type question would be, What are the propositions which will account for deviant behavior? Studies of specific cases will be conducted, to be sure, but once the generalizations have been drawn from the studies, they will then be "applied" in some manner to explain and predict the deviancy of individuals not included in the studies. The educationist might ask, What is the learning difficulty of a particular student? He would then turn to his own research or that of the psychologists to find certain principles of learning. His "treatment" of the student's learning difficulty would then be done in terms of those principles. In short, what I am saying is that education has been sociologistic in that it has been, and still is, nomothetic in its approach to individuals.

Bressler, a sociologist, has argued the opposite,[7] asserting that the conventional wisdom of education has predisposed the educationists to be idiographic rather than nomothetic in his approach to the problems of his field of inquiry. His argument is based on the frequent usage by the educationists of such statements as "A person is not a statistic." True, educational literature is liberally sprinkled with talk of individual differences, of individualizing instruction, of getting to know the student as person, etc., but when educational researchers do speak of these matters, it is in nomothetic terms. Individual differences, for example, are treated as plot points on one or more theoretical or empirical distributions. Hence, even though educationists do speak frequently in terms which appear to be idiographic, they, in fact, are not. Even though they say many nice things about individual students, educationists, like sociologists, are nomothetic in their explanations of human action, for they do not have the linguistic and conceptual tools for talking about education as a first-person experience.

The nomothetic approach to the study and explanation of human action is not limited to educationists and sociologists. As I have already indicated, it is an approach and an attitude and a philosophic bias and a methodological bias which permeates our entire culture, predisposing us to studying human action always in terms of some law, principle, or method. The first step in finding radically new perspectives from which to study man may be simply in becoming aware of this cultural bias. The sociological-nomothetic orientation has us so locked into our mental boxes that thinkers such as Dostoevsky and Nietzsche may be still considered ahead of, not just their time, but ours as well. Mora, in comparing human manipulation in the Soviet Union and the West,[8] points out clearly that, in pointing accusing fingers at the Soviets, Westerners have been unaware of their own manipulation of individuals in terms of *apriori* conceptions of the good society and of knowledge. This is just one example of the consequences of our not being aware of our own sociological-nomothetic orientation.

Other examples are not difficult to find. A prime value in the broad spectrum of the American middle class is for the individual to find his niche, his spot, and to adapt his needs to those of the society. And most of these niches have already been identified and labelled, making it possible for the sociologist to speak at length of roles, institutions, social classes, power structures, etc., without giving any consideration to the individual's phenomenological view of either himself or of his social world. Should a person choose to define himself in such a manner as to deny the validity of any of society's niches for his own life, he would be declared deviant and, to the delight of the sociologist, still be classifiable in one of those vaguely defined categories such as creative genius or sociopath. Such a person would, to quote one of my students, "give a computer a stomach ache." Educationists, with a few rare exceptions, have followed the same approach in speaking of students in the schools. The roles, the niches, have already been determined, and the student is expected to fit into the previously determined structure or else be declared deviant. One example will illustrate the point. In a recent book, *Sociology and Education,*[9] Stalcup devoted all of two and one-half pages to the subject of students in the schools, and there the discussion is entirely in terms of "position," "social structure," "clique structure," and "groups." Stalcup is not atypical at all in his approach; for his work reflects the typical sociological-nomothetic bias found in most of the literature of education.

The consequence of the sociological-nomothetic bias of

11

our culture which this author sees as being the consequence of greatest magnitude and effect is that of alienation. The topic of alienation was raised to the level of major philosophic importance by Hegel in his *Phenomenology of Mind,* but, in the ordinary experience of the man-on-the-street, alienation is felt as a dissatisfaction with our affluent society and by the university student as a feeling that his education is completely irrelevant to what he values in life. Hegel saw alienation to be the condition of being not at one with Mind; this was not merely a feeling of the individual. Rather, this was an objective state of affairs in which even Nature itself was alienated, cut off, from Mind. Further, each of man's creations, Hegel's "alienation of creativity," takes him away from that state of at-oneness with Mind, which is the state free from alienation. If one substitutes the term *God* for the term *Mind,* as some Protestant theologians have done, one can use Hegel's conception of alienation as a dogma of original sin.

Marx very quickly saw the central function of alienation in human life but substituted for Hegel's "alienation of creativity" the "alienation of productivity" which eventually was transformed into the "alienation of labor." Marx saw that the products of man's endeavors—technology, markets, and property-systems—were acquiring greater priority than man himself and that man was coming to see these as forces of life to which he must bow in acceptance. Thus, those in command of such a system of priorities could convince ordinary man that he, ordinary man, really had no life connection with those products. In effect, man is alienated from the labor of his own hands. For Marx, then, alienation was not man from Mind, as in Hegel, but man from the products of his labor. Man was literally selling his hands. The solutions to the problem proposed by Marx and his followers have been so unacceptable to American ears that we have overlooked his very perceptive analysis of the problem itself.

Although the thinking of philosophers, such as Hegel and Marx, regarding the matter of alienation has generated little acceptance in this country, especially among philosophers of education, the existential fact of alienation remains. The feeling of estrangement to ourselves and others, the inarticulable visceral dissonances, the clumsiness of our attempts at communication, the frightening awareness of the superficiality of most social intercourse, the sense of being lost in a rapidly changing world, the weariness of never being a significant factor in those changes—all these and more testify to the presence of alienation without making any claims regarding the objective nature of alienation, if such there be. Neither the Hegelian claim, nor that of the religionist, nor the Marxian one is acceptable to us, yet the feelings of alienation are still very present with us.

A major portion of the blame can be assigned to the sociological-nomothetic bias of our culture. The bias operates in our methods of researching human action, in our theories of man and society, and in our organization of industry and education. By this I mean that the operation is always from previously determined methods, principles, laws, structures to the individual. Granted that feedback from individuals involved does occur and is allowed, but structure is primary and remains basically intact. In most research, the individual is merely another variable to be manipulated; in the usual theories of man and society, the individual is secondary to the logical requirements for a good theory; and in the organization of industry and education, the laborer and the student are invariably stuck at the bottom of the organizational charts-of-power. Our society probably is not as far from Hegel and Marx as we would like to think. Sociology reigns, and the feelings subsumed under the term *alienation* multiply.

If the sense of being alienated is a fact among the members of our society—more specifically, if the sense of being alienated is a very pervasive one among students and teachers, could one not remedy this feeling-of-being-cut-off-from by grounding the educational institutions and other agencies of the society in the lived experiences of the individuals involved. In other words, would an approach to the study of man and the arrangements of social relationships grounded in man's ordinary experience reduce the feelings of alienation? Although the question of alienation and its reduction is not the major focus of this work, the author would answer "yes" to the question, for the circumstances described in expressions of alienation are those possible only in a sociologically-nomothetically arranged society.

Phenomenologists, including the existentialists for the

13

moment, have given considerable attention to the matter of alienation, not as a primary topic in itself, but as one related to the larger problem of the possibilities of beginning inquiry into man within the experiential world of man himself. Phenomenology sees philosophy, not as a science of reason, but as an analysis of the progressively achieved awareness of what its means to be an intending-body; that is, what does it mean to be conscious, to be free, to be responsible, to be historical? As Edie puts it, "Phenomenology is neither a science of objects nor a science of subjects; it is a science of *experience.*"[10] From this definition one might conclude that phenomenology is a *radical empiricism* in the manner of William James, who also established immediate experience as the starting point of his inquiry. If this were the case, then perhaps two alternatives to the sociological-nomothetic approach are already available: phenomenology and *radical empiricism.* But James' thought, for all its original insights, was identified very quickly with pragmatism, which was, from the beginning, nomothetic. Advocates of phenomenology, on the other hand, continue to argue that phenomenology is the very science of experience. Schrader, for example, asserts that

> Without severe distortion we may simply observe that phenomenology since Hegel has been concerned to offer a descriptive account of human experience as it is directly encountered. It may be viewed, therefore, as a particularly inclusive type of empiricism.[11]

But phenomenology has never been content to remain at the level of "human experience as it is directly encountered." Husserl, very early, developed a phenomenology as thoroughly idealistic as any Hegelianism. For Husserl, as set forth in his *Ideas: General Introduction to Pure Phenomenology,*[12] the object of phenomenology is to determine the essence of things themselves. One arrives at the knowledge of things themselves through a process of *epoche,* a process of suspending judgment. *Epoche* is accomplished by *bracketing.* In *bracketing,* one severs from the field of consciousness all preconceived ideas, beliefs, biases, etc., thus allowing the *eidetic reduction;* that is, a getting to the base, the essence, of the thing in question by excluding from con-

14

sciousness all perceptual biases, explanatory constructs, etc. Such a reduction, according to Husserl, results in knowledge of the essence of things themselves, not of factual properties, but of essential being. Husserl became more and more concerned with the nature of essential being, resulting in his giving primary attention to the nature of Being, knowledge of which one could gain through *transcendental reduction*, which brackets out all but pure consciousness and what is given to it. Individual being came to be seen, then, as merely the reflection of, the working through, an expression of, Being. Husserl gave to phenomenology an approach to man which still dominates phenomenological method, namely, an emphasis on ontological Being at the expense of ontic (empirical) being.

Cairns,[13] in summarizing the propositions which would be acceptable to Husserl and to most phenomenologists and which would distinguish them from other philosophers, unwittingly illustrates the point that, although phenomenology claims to be the science of human experience, it actually is concerned more with abstract universals. For example, on one hand Cairns says that the correct fundamental procedure in philosophizing is a process of attending to affairs that are presented, then explicating them with respect to such of their determinations and relations as are likewise presented and grasped, while, on the other hand, he says that real individuals exemplify ideal universals. He further states that propositions about universals point to "an ideally possible verification or refutation by a grasping and analyzing of universals themselves and by an observing of the limits beyond which an entity plainly could not vary while remaining a self-consistent member of the ideal extension of its universal essence." [14] Phenomenology, thus, remains the science of experience only by redefining experience out of its individual human meaning. Experience becomes simply another idealistic universal, and "human experience as it is directly encountered" ceases to be the primary focus.

A few writers have attempted to find in phenomenology "implications" for education, have attempted to find in phenomenology a way of dealing with educational phenomena from the perspective of the individual. One book in particular, Snygg and Combs' *Individual Behavior*,[15] has had considerable influence in certain educational circles, especially among guidance and counseling personnel. What they attempted was to set forth an "applied" phenomenology, a phenomenological approach to the explanation of human behavior and to the counseling of students and clients. That they were charting new territory in counseling psychology is to be recognized, and that they were seeking a non-mechanistic, non-nomothetic way of explaining human behavior is to be commended. But, their effort to use phenomenology as their philosophic springboard resulted in a work containing the same problem as that in phenomenology itself, as pointed out in the preceding paragraph. Individual behavior, as a major premise, is inconsistent with Husserl's pure phenomenology.

It may be argued that Snygg and Combs were not attempting a "pure phenomenology," that they were striving for a phenomenological theory appropriate to the needs of personnel in "helping relationships." If that be the case, a detailed analysis, independent of any concern with phenomenology, is called for. Such analysis has been done by Beck [16] who, though quite in sympathy with their attempt, finds their reasoning woefully weak. One example of Beck's analysis will be sufficient to illustrate the point. For Snygg and Combs choice is a pseudo-concept; the individual does what he does in any given situation in order to either 1) maintain himself, or 2) enhance himself. Now, asks Beck, how are we to explain counselor behavior, for the counselor, also, does what he must do in every utterance he makes, to maintain and enhance his phenomenal self. The counselor, in fact, cannot even choose which theory of counseling he will follow, for that too will be determined by his maintenance and enhancement needs. Beck offers additional criticism of the same point by arguing that Snygg and Combs do not provide for the confirmability, even in principle, of the hypothesis that one's phenomenal field precludes genuine choice. He concludes the argument by stating that the hypothesis is tautological, that it is tantamount to saying that "A man takes the course of action that he takes." The criticisms notwithstanding, the influence of *Individual Behavior* continues. But neither a philosophy of education nor a set of guides to educational practice can be grounded on reasoning as flawed as theirs.

Tenenbaum [17] has attempted to deal specifically with the matter of phenomenological implications for education. His main emphasis derives from certain assumptions regarding the uniqueness of individual perceptions; his main criticism is directed toward mechanistic conceptions of mind and learning; and, his main proposal consists of an insistence that education become genuinely student-centered as opposed to the present teacher and subject matter centeredness. But, while Tenenbaum's thinking is oriented toward phenomenological concerns, neither his main emphasis, nor his main criticism, nor his main proposal is derived from phenomenological method or presuppositions. Rather, his thinking appears to be grounded more in ordinary experience than in Husserlian phenomenology.

If we are to talk of education as first-person experience, we must first provide sound reasons for defining education in such a manner, and, then, be prepared to follow out certain of the implications of such definition. To do the first of these let us focus on ordinary experience as the starting point for our inquiry into the nature of education and, if necessary, develop the language and concepts for talking of education from the perspective of ordinary experience. If this can be accomplished, then perhaps we can establish sounder grounds for the proposals of such writers as Tenenbaum.

From Phenomenology to Ordinary Experience

If both phenomenology and ordinary experience are concerned with the lived experience of individuals, wherein do they differ? A beginning answer is found in Edie's comment that "Heidegger begins where Dostoevsky, Nietzsche, Kierkegaard, Malraux, and Camus end." [18] By this Edie means that Heidegger is more concerned with the ontological than with the ontic, the empirical. As pointed out earlier, phenomenology became almost totally preoccupied with the ontological, with the problem of the nature of Being. Ordinary experience, on the other hand, is a more radical empiricism, for its primary concerns revolve about the perceptual-feeling-becoming world of the individual, that world which was the special concern of Nietzsche, Kierkegaard, and Camus. No one of these three, however, developed a radical grounding of education in the lived experience of individuals. Kaelin [19] has stated that when philosophy does become thoroughly radical, the process will be that of the reflective being thinking about his non-reflective states, that is, to expand on Kaelin, the pre-predicative, pre-conceptual relations of *Dasein* with the world, which are the conditions of lived experience. Hence, although ordinary experience draws insights from phenomenology, it is much closer to common sense than to pure phenomenology. By common sense, I do not mean a naive realism or a "being natural," but, rather, what one might say if asked to "stop and think" about his world for the first time.

Just as Merleau-Ponty found that the primary difficulty in his work was in the possibility of a philosophy of perception without getting outside of perception, so it is the primary difficulty, perhaps stumbling block to the rationalists, to develop a philosophy of education without getting outside the phenomenological domain of education. And, just what is that domain? The ordinary experience of the individuals involved. Although coming at the matter from an entirely different perspective, McLuhan pointed specifically to ordinary experience when he said that "what is meant by the irrational and non-logical in much modern discussions is merely the rediscovery of ordinary transactions between the self and the world." [20] One of the things McLuhan is saying, among others, is that modern man does not have available to him concepts for talking about ordinary experience; thus, when he attempts to reflect on his non-reflective states, he is forced to use such terms as irrational and non-logical.

To further clarify what is meant by the phenomenological domain of education, consider the case of a student in a class which is dealing with time in terms of velocity and acceleration. The instructor has placed the appropriate formulas on the board with accompanying explanation, but, while considering these concepts, the student may be experiencing something quite different in respect to time. He may be bored and think that the class has lasted an eternity, or he may become quite involved with the material and feel frustrated at the shortness of time available. In the same total experience he is probably getting conflicting signals as to the nature of time. In respect to the education of that particular student, which "time" is more real? If we consider the student's "other" sense of time as being an important variable for which we must account in a theory of instruction, we run into the difficulty of not possessing the linguistic and conceptual tools for talking about such experience.

Culkin provides another example of the inadequacies of available language and concepts for talking about lived experiences.

> While lecturing to a large audience in a modern hotel in Chicago, a distinguished professor is bitten in the leg by a cobra. The whole experience takes three seconds. He is affected through the touch of the reptile, the gasp of the crowd, the swimming sights before his eyes. His memory, imagination, and emotions come into emergency action. A lot of things happen in three seconds. Two weeks later he is fully recovered and wants to write up the experience in a letter to a colleague. To communicate this experience through print means that it must first be broken down into parts and then mediated, eye-dropper fashion, one thing at a time, in an abstract, linear, fragmented, sequential way. That is the essential structure of print. And once a culture uses such a medium for a few centuries, it begins to perceive the world in a one-thing-at-a-time, abstract, linear, fragmented, sequential way. And it shapes its organizations and schools according to the same premises.[21]

The phenomenological domain of education, what I have called ordinary experience, is this domain of experiential, simultaneous, multidimensional happening. The language for theoretical and philosophical work in education must be one which will be adequate for talking about the lived experience of the individuals who make up the process. Such language must not only permit us to talk of behaviors, and objective roles, and public verifiability, but must also equip us to talk meaningfully about such experiential matters as individual perceptions, subjectivity, aesthetic feelings, multi-levels of awareness, the all-at-onceness of experiences, and about authentication of information. To dismiss such matters as being merely "emotive" ones is to foster still

19

more alienation and disenchantment within and without the educational enterprise. The psychologist with his mathematical models of behavior can ignore such matters; the sociologist with his role theories can; so can the philosopher with his objective epistemologies; but the philosopher *of education,* because of the phenomenological nature of education, cannot.

If one begins his inquiry into education at the domain of ordinary experience, does he not preclude ever freeing himself from, as Saunders and Henze have called it,[22] the egocentric predicament? If one begins with his own case, with his own experiential data of the present moment, is it possible to escape the predicament? Or is it really a predicament at all? Those whom Saunders and Henze have called the egocentric philosophers would not see the matter as being a predicament, for they find the problem to be simply one of how to get from this experiential, private knowledge to knowledge of others, a problem which they handle in a variety of ways. The nonegocentric philosophers would not see the matter as being a predicament, for they reject the very notion of an experiential, private knowledge; hence, the whole matter is, in fact, not a genuine problem at all. The nonegocentric philosopher is concerned, rather, with clarifying the public standards of justification used in science and everyday life. Arguing from a Wittgensteinian position, Saunders and Henze set out to analyze various arguments which have been put forward by egocentric philosophers. They finally conclude by claiming that all such arguments can be defeated, provided that the egocentric philosophers are not permitted "a concept of *myself* and *my* experience" [23] (italics theirs). But to deny that I can talk about myself and my experiences is to redefine me as something other than human. What they are saying is that, for their argument to be effective, they must squeeze out of the argument that which the argument is about. They have in a very sophisticated, yet unaware way, illustrated the sociological-nomothetic problem of attempting to talk of individuals. For the arguments of nonegocentric philosophers to hold, they must talk about something other than the ordinary experience of the individual. It was in reaction against Hegelian philosophy that Kierkegaard once commented that " 'The individual' is the category through which this age,

all history, the human race as a whole must pass." [24] Inquiry
into education must begin in ordinary experience, for it is
of the nature of first person experience that all history, all
knowledge will pass. Of course, grave problems are encountered in this assertion, but a philosophy rooted in
experience and directed toward the analysis of experience
is not amenable to logical vivisection as that is typically
practiced in Anglo-American philosophy. On several occa-
sions Albert Camus was criticized for contaminating his
logic with experiential evidence and with his "emotional
attitude." He rarely replied, even though the criticisms
came from philosophers of the stature of A. J. Ayer. One
of Camus' friends, however, could not let the attacks go by
without reply. That friend, Chiaromonte, replied by showing
that Camus refused to give answers simply because logical
ones were available.[25] He continued his defense by arguing
that if the diversity and contradictions of human experience
transcend logical categories, then logic is to be ignored.
Compulsive attempts to logically categorize human experience may be evasions of the real problems of human experience. Chiaromonte concludes by saying that all such
categories as Reason and Unreason are attempts to jump
out of the real problem by giving it a final solution. Although most Anglo-American philosophers have forgotten,
philosophers of education must not forget that human experience, at least in our domain of inquiry, takes priority.
With Camus, we must assert the priority of individual
experience.

Goodman [26] asserts that education should be grounded in
individual experience and makes that assertion on the basis
of social rather than philosophic grounds. What he is offering is not a contradictory premise, but supporting evidence
for the proposition of this work, namely, that the theories
and rationales of education must be grounded in ordinary
experience. He points out that the conditions of modern
social and technological organization are so pervasively and
rigidly conforming, it has become necessary for education
to assist in fostering human initiative by protecting the
young from top-down direction. The public schools, he says,
"regiment individuals and rigidify class stratification."
Viewing Goodman's statements from the perspective of
this work, one could conclude that the state of affairs is

one of the outcomes of attempts to construct philosophies of education on sociological, nonegocentric premises.

Comparative Presuppositions of Language

The study of education has been conducted with borrowed languages (linguistic and conceptual tools), languages which are behavioristic, objective, and referential. Although the languages used in the study of education have been borrowed from a variety of disciplines, most of the languages have come from the lexicons of psychology, sociology, and philosophy. From psychology has come the language of quantification of muscle movements; from sociology, the language of objective role theory; and, from Anglo-American philosophy, language-tools for the analysis of language. Hence, we have come to talk about learning and teaching in terms of specific behaviors and sets of behaviors, about the relationships in the educative process in terms of objective role relationships, and about the language of education itself in terms of referential theories of meaning.[27] As a result of the use of such languages, to teach has come to mean effective specification and programming; to know, to make appropriate responses; to evaluate, to determine the number of correct responses needed to judge a performance to be a good one; to organize and administer, to pattern after business and industrial models. All of this is but to say in different terms what was said earlier in the chapter, namely, that education has been studied primarily with the linguistic and conceptual tools of sociology, as that term has been defined in this chapter. In borrowing the language-tools of sociology, education has also adopted the implied presuppositions of such tools, that is, perceptual sets toward, prescriptions for, and assumptions about the study of education itself. The purpose of this section, then, is 1) to make apparent the presuppositions of sociological-nomothetic language, and 2) to set forth, in the beginning of the work, the presuppositions of the language of ordinary experience. Chapter Two will explicate the first, and Chapters Three and Four, the second.

1. The presuppositions of sociological-nomothetic language are seven in number.

a. The order is linear. The requirement of linearity is

evidenced by the grammatical demands of declarative sentences, by the number systems of statistical procedures, and by the sequential order entailed in certain explanations of causality.

b. The motive is to obtain explanatory theories; this is evidenced by the demand that any putative science to be a genuine science must go beyond the descriptive level to that of explanation.

c. The "logics" are those of inference and implication. This refers to the standardized rules for dealing with empirical data and major propositions.

d. The process is reductionistic. The process of atomizing, of breaking that under investigation into its smallest component units, is almost universal in sociological-nomothetic types of research, types which dominate in education. Even studies in group processes are primarily concerned with analysis of, i. e., reduction of, the processes into smaller, more understandable units, understandable, that is, in terms of their explanatory theories.

e. The determinism is historical. The assumption is that, given knowledge of antecedent conditions, the present consequences can be understood. This assumption is quite obvious in studies of social deviancy, explanations of learning difficulties, and in the school counselor's use of cumulative records.

f. The goal is to be rational. Whether one holds to an *a priori* or *a posteriori* conception of knowledge, both rationalists and empiricists have insisted that nomothetic explanations are to be sought.

g. The criterion is verifiability. The assumption is that if a given statement is coherent with other previously-accepted-as-true statements, or refers, not to other statements, but to observable states of affairs, or can be checked out against other data by other observers, that statement is true.

2. The presuppositions of the language of ordinary experience can also be stated in seven sentences.

a. The order is simultaneous; this is to say that the language of ordinary experience recognizes and attempts to account for the non-linear, all-at-onceness of lived experience.

b. The motive is to obtain awareness of field relationships. If such awareness leads to explanatory theories, fine, but it is assumed that much of human experience—including much of that special slice of human experience called education—is of a once-for-all nature and, hence, is not amenable to explanatory models.

c. The "logic" is that of metaphorical parallels. The assumption is that, at best, much of human knowing consists, not of inferences and implications, but of the drawing of parallels between and among the experiences of others.

d. The process is organic; this is to say that much of human experience, perhaps all of that which can be identified as first-person experience, occurs in an idiographic, gestalt manner.

e. The determinism is episodic. The reality of antecedents is not denied; rather, the assumption is that the determinants of meaning of a particular episode of experience are significantly present in the episode itself.

f. The goal is to be reasonable. The term *reasonable* is used to differentiate the role of reason in the language of ordinary experience from the rationalistic tradition, on the one hand, and from certain contemporary irrationalist movements, on the other. Reason, in this context, possesses tool value, meaning that it is useful for developing notions of the world, which allow us to live effectively in the world, but is not useful in setting forth either large conceptual schemes or comprehensive methods for explaining all of experience.

g. The criterion is personal authentication. While it may be meaningful, in any one of several senses, to speak of public verification of "out there" facts and/or events, for the facts or events to take on personal significance—that is, become first-person experience—individual appropriation to one's own life becomes necessary.

It is quite obvious that these seven presuppositions of the language of ordinary experience generate, at this point, more difficulties than solutions and that extensive explication is required. Such explication is the major task of this work.

To This Point

The effort to this point has been to provide a preliminary definition of the concept *ordinary experience* and to locate, through excursions into and criticisms of sociological-nomothetic and phenomenological thought, the role of the concept in the study of education.

Chapter II

LANGUAGE ANALYSIS IN EDUCATION

Introduction

Conceptions of language analysis used in the clarification and explication of educational discourse have, in the main, been those of the mainstream of contemporary Anglo-American philosophy. That mainstream has consisted of several different subcurrents—the Positivism of the Vienna Circle, the thinking of which can be represented by such people as Carnap and Ayer; Logical Atomism, represented by Russell; Pragmatism, by Peirce; and, Ordinary Language Analysis, represented by such philosophers as the later Wittgenstein and Ryle. This last current of thought, Ordinary Language Analysis, is the major one in Anglo-American philosophy today, including the work of philosophers in education. Among these subcurrents are to be found different techniques of analysis and disagreements regarding what should be the primary focus of the analyses. For example, some have been primarily concerned with the syntax of language, that is, with the formal relations among the signs themselves; others have focused on the problem of semantics, that is, what do the signs signify, point to; while yet others have concerned themselves with the effects of signs, that is, with the pragmatics of language.

Yet, for all the differences in techniques and points of focus, all share certain things in common. Language analysts assert, for example, that philosophy should investigate language itself, for it is language which has created most of the traditional problems of philosophy. Philosophers should, in other words, clean their glasses before saying what the world looks like. Perhaps, philosophers should not say what the world looks like at all, but, rather, should limit themselves completely to the matter of obtaining "clean glasses;" that is, perhaps we should redefine philosophy as the discipline of language analysis. Another commonality is the emphasis on clarity of definition, the meaning of 'definition,' and the procedures for determining definitions. Another commonality is the requirement of exactness of use; precision of language is an ultimate good for the language analyst. These and other commonalities will be discussed in detail in a later section of the chapter, but the mention of these three indicates that, although procedures and foci of analysis differ, certain larger considerations permit discussion of contemporary Anglo-American philosophic analysis under the same rubric.

Such analysis in education has been of considerable help in the clarification of policy statements, in the elimination of much jargon, in determining the meaningfulness, if any, of certain educational slogans and favorite rallying cries, and in the explication of key terms in the teaching-learning process, terms such as need, and motivation, and achievement. Several analyses of these matters will be discussed in this chapter. The thrust of this chapter is not to deny the contributions of Anglo-American philosophic analysis, but is, rather, to offer criticisms to the effect that, because of the experiential nature of education, language itself must be conceived of in broader terms and the procedures for the analysis of language must be modified to take into account this conception of education.

Typical Analyses in Education

To provide the background for the critique to follow, four types of analysis used in education will be illustrated: 1) the uncovering of hidden premises; 2) the clarification of syntactic relations using symbolic logic; 3) the clarification of meaning through the use of referential criteria; and, 4) clarification with criteria-of-use. No special validity is claimed for this typology. The last three are, quite obviously, classified on the basis that they are different techniques of analysis. The first, however, may use any one or combination of the last three, for it is not a class of technique but one of purpose. The only validity claimed for the classification is that these four are the types of analytic

27

works found frequently in the literature of philosophy of education.

1) An excellent example of the uncovering of hidden premises is to be found in the paper, "The Suppressed Premiss in Educational Psychology," by Edward Best.[1] Operating very much in the mainstream of Anglo-American philosophy, Best begins with a reference to Hume's distinction between "is" sentences and "ought" sentences. After accepting this distinction without question, he points out that to jump from one type of sentence to the other would be intolerable in the physical sciences but that it is done frequently in the literature of educational psychology. He then analyzes out the prescriptive terms in each of four sentences taken from works in educational psychology, indicating that, if the author meant "This brings about that," the word *should* is not prescriptive. On the other hand, if the author meant "This is what the teacher ought to do," the word is prescriptive. Perhaps the educational psychologists do have certain aims in mind, and Best attempts to find them. But what he finds are vague, ambiguous sentences which the advocates of almost any type of society or person could accept. His conclusion is that educational psychologists have not provided statements of aims which are in any way logically related to the findings of their research; hence, their "should" sentences are to be read as prescriptive ones. Best then turns to the analysis of the writings of certain leading psychologists in learning theory, educational statistics, and testing. And his conclusion is the same. The suppressed premise in educational psychology is the prescriptive one.

2) It has been long argued, particularly by the positivists, that, to avoid semantic paradoxes, a formalized language, such as symbolic logic, must be developed. In other words, an ideal language, designed so as not to generate paradoxes and other difficulties, is needed for the analysis of ordinary language—a "pure semantics" to distinguish it from "empirical semantics." The practical, "empirical" nature of education has tended to preclude very much serious attention to the argument. One writer, however, has argued that a "logic of instruction" will have to utilize symbolic logic in its formulation. That writer, Mosier,[2] affirms with the enthusiasm of the new convert

28

that it is symbolic logic which will "profoundly influence our conceptions of philosophic analysis in the domain of education," that symbolic logic is the "powerful analytic weapon with which to attack the problems of education," and that it is his task to persuade his colleagues in education to apply the techniques of symbolic logic. Ignoring his exhortations, let us look at his argument.

Mosier argues that the inquiry logic of Dewey was a logic of learning, not a logic of instruction; the experience of the learner, but not that of the teacher, was accounted for in inquiry logic. What is experienced in a symbol is a complex, and this is accounted for in inquiry logic, but what is represented in a symbol is a concept, and this is not. However, one does not, according to Mosier, exclude the other, for together they constitute an integration, which he defines as mutual implication, expressed thusly, p ↔ q, a term which means p if, and only if, q. With this schema, then, we may determine the truth-value of sentences purporting to say something about the teaching-learning process. Mosier concludes by saying that the consequences of an object experienced, which is essential to learning, are the starting point of knowing the object as represented, which is essential to teaching and that symbolic logic, as the logic of instruction, provides the language-tools for clarifying the relation between the two as well as re-emphasizing conceptual thought in the educative process.

3) Referential methods of language analysis range from the approaches of Korzybski [3] and Hayakawa [4] to those of Morris [5] and Ayer.[6] The simplest referential criterion is that if a sign has extensional significance, that is, if it points to some objective referent in the world, then it is a meaningful sign. Morris improves on this by pointing out the problems with the meaning of meaning and also by using acts as referents rather than things. Since the most sophisticated treatment has been that of Ayer and since he has dealt with some of the major problems confronted by philosophers of education, the attention will be given to his work.

We may state Ayer's general criterion in this way: a sentence which does not express either a formally true proposition or an empirical hypothesis is devoid of literal significance. By this, Ayer means that a sentence, which

29

makes any contribution to knowledge, must be either a tautology or one which is immediately or potentially verifiable, with verifiability being defined in empirical-referential terms. A tautology is defined as a sentence constructed from other sentences in such a way that the sentence in question has a calculated truth value for every possible assignment of truth values to the original sentences. As such, a tautology contributes to knowledge, not by introducing new matters of fact, but by telling us something about that which is already known. But it is not the tautology with which Ayer is primarily concerned. He is concerned with the bulk of meaningful sentences, namely, those that are empirically verifiable. It should be noted, at this point, that Ayer is quite aware of the problems of speaking of meaningfulness, and generally avoids the term, and he is also aware that definitions are not of things but are of uses.

To clarify what he means by the method of verification, let us look at his use of that method in the resolution of two philosophic problems germane to education. One of these is the traditional conflict between rationalism and empiricism; the other, between realism and idealism. The first is germane to education at the points of epistemology, theories of curriculum construction, and educational research. The second is germane if for no other reason than that most philosophy of education textbooks still, in one way or another, pit these two against each other.

The first of these problems, that between rationalism and empiricism, is posed by Ayer in this manner. Rationalists, according to him, have held that there exists a "supra-sensible" world which is the object of intellectual intuition.[7] From this world certain first principles or *a priori* propositions are intuited and, from these, deductions can be made concerning matters of fact. Empiricists reject this, contending that a proposition can only have factual content if it is subject to empirical verification. Strict empiricists have insisted that one of the criteria of empirical verification must be that all propositions of matters of fact must be conclusively verifiable. As can be readily seen, this problem is both an epistemological and a metaphysical one. Hume, as such an empiricist, would say, according to Ayer, that man passively waits for nature to instruct him, whereas the rationalist would argue that man is active in knowledge; he forces nature to answer his questions. To restate the problem, the rationalist's world of truth is "out there" to be actively sought by mind; this is to be contrasted with the empiricist's world of sense-data impinging on the organism. In his resolution of the problem, Ayer agrees that statements of matters of fact must be verified empirically; on the other hand, he rejects the notion that there are no propositions which are valid apart from all experience. Tautologies, as defined, are true because of what they do, not because of any claimed metaphysical grounding. Furthermore, a scientist may consider the possibility of a law long before he possesses the evidence needed to justify the law. Intuition, therefore, is not rejected, but its meaning is clarified; that is, it is shown to be a psychological question, How does our knowledge originate? rather than the logical one, How is it certified as knowledge? [8] Hence, the rationalist-empiricist argument is resolved by clarifying what is meant by tautology, by intuition, and by empirical verification.

The second traditional argument which Ayer analyzes, and which is being summarized here to illustrate his method, is that between realism and idealism.[9] The basic question which divided the two is, Do sense contents exist independent of the knower? The idealists have answered "no" while the realists have answered "yes." Ayer states that the logical doctrines maintained by idealists and controverted by realists are all concerned with the question, What is entailed by sentences of the form "x is real"? Berkeleyan idealists contend that "x is real" is equivalent to "x exists" which is equivalent to "x is perceived" which is equivalent to "x is mental." They conclude that everything that exists is mental. Berkeley held that a thing is nothing more than the sum of its sensible qualities and that it was self-contradictory to assert that a sensible thing existed unsensed. Other idealists have argued that "x is real" is equivalent to "x is thought of;" hence, it is self-contradictory to hold that anything exists unthought of. The realists reject any notion that the known is contingent upon being known, in any sense, and contend that things do exist whether known or not.

Ayer attempts to resolve the dispute by first pointing out that a thing is to be defined, not as a collection of sense contents, but as a logical construction out of them. Secondly, he points out that the elements of any given material are not merely actual but also possible sense-contents. That is, the sentences referring to a material thing need not express categorical propositions; they may be hypothetical. Ayer, thus, resolves the dispute between the realists and idealists by stating that there is no contradiction involved in asserting the existence of a material thing which is never actually perceived, for, in asserting that the thing existed, one would only be asserting that certain sense-contents would occur if a particular set of conditions relating to the faculties of the position of an observer was fulfilled. He uses Mill's conception of a material thing as "a permanent possibility of sensation" in this solution.

4) Ordinary language analysts attempt to approach problems of language—paradoxes, ambiguities, multiple meanings, etc.—as free of prior definitions and criteria of meaning as possible. What they do attempt is to sort out the many uses of words and sentences as a way of clarifying the intended meaning and of increasing the effectiveness of communication. In addition to this activity of clarification, they also attempt to establish standards of use by developing paradigm cases. Such paradigm cases are built up from the previously mentioned process of sorting out the various uses of a term. For a field of endeavor as complex and varied as that subsumed under the term *education*, ordinary language analysis has much to offer, and the greater portion of philosophic analysis in education is now of this type. For one who is familiar at all with the literature in education, the need for clarification and standardization seems apparent. The statements and pronouncements which have developed about the terms "freedom" and "discipline," motivational terms such as impulse and drive, metaphors adopted from the physical sciences, concepts of maturation and achievement, terms such as intelligence and rationality, the thousand and one lists of educational objectives—all these, and more, appear very much in need of clarification. To illustrate how such clarification is done, four analyses will be summarized. The four are by Scheffler, Roland, Peters, and Komisar and Coombs.

a) In Chapter Five of his book, *The Language of Education*,[10] Scheffler does an analysis of "teaching" and "telling" based on three pairs of schemata, each pair comprised of a schema paradigmatic of some use of "to teach" and another schema paradigmatic of a corresponding use of "to tell."

A. X tells Y that . . .
B. X teaches Y that . . . .
C. X tells Y to . . .
D. X teaches Y to . . .
E. X tells Y how to . . .
F. X teaches Y how to . . .

In a discussion of A (telling that) and B (teaching that), Scheffler points out that telling, like teaching, may involve trying, but unlike teaching, it does not generally involve X's trying to get Y to learn. Thus, if X is successful in teaching Y that Columbus discovered America, X learns that Columbus discovered America. On the other hand, if X is successful in telling Y that Columbus discovered America, we cannot infer that Y has learned that fact. Now, if teaching has occurred, how long must Y retain the fact? The answer to this, according to Scheffler, is not completely relevant to the immediate question, but does point up incidentally why testing is relevant to teaching but not to telling. If a test of the student shows no retention, it may be reasonable to infer that teaching has not taken place. Under the same circumstances, however, the telling might be quite successful.

With regard to A and B, Scheffler introduces a line of thought which touches on a point of considerable puzzlement to educators and of disputation among philosophers. He begins by referring to such sentences as "Columbus discovered America" as fact-stating sentences. He then contends that his A and B schema may take, not only fact-stating sentences, but norm-stating sentences as well; for example, "One ought to pay one's debts," or "Honesty is the best policy." Thus, Scheffler contends that we may speak of telling someone that he ought to pay his debts, or of teaching someone that honesty is the best policy. And, he contends this in the face of much criticism to the effect that normative statements cannot be analyzed in the manner of fact-statements. He admits that the problem of verificaion is a grave and difficult one with norm-statements. By putting his case into behavioral terms, however, he attempts to demonstrate some degree of verifiability for norm-statements. He illustrates this with the case of a fellow named Jones who is said to have learned that honesty is the best policy. If he has really learned this, we may suppose that Jones has acquired a pattern of behavior which is known as being honest. Success in teaching comes to imply a sort of norm-acquisition which it did not before with respect to fact-statements. For X to have been successful in teaching Y that honesty is the best policy comes to imply something not implied by X's success in teaching Y that Columbus discovered America. Success in teaching may now be tested by seeing if Y's conduct conforms to the norm in question.

The C and D schema requires imperatives as blank-fillers. The independence of teaching from telling is illustrated quite clearly by Scheffler in his discussion of statements of the forms C and D. For example, to teach someone to appreciate Bach, to understand quantum theory, to enjoy ballet, to sympathize with the poor, is quite different from telling him to do so. In such cases, "telling to" may actually hinder the "teaching to."

Scheffler points out in his treatment of the E and F forms that sentences of the type F are easily confused with sentences of type D. He notes that, although D and F are two different kinds of sentences, the D form can be used as an abbreviation of an F form sentence. For example, to teach someone to do arithmetic problems is to teach him how to do them. Not all sentences of the F form, however, can be stated in the D form. Consider, for example, "X teaches Y to pay his debts." This is not the same as "X teaches Y how to pay his debts." The first of these may refer to character training, while the second refers to the techniques of check-writing, etc. Consideration of this example illustrates Scheffler's point that teaching someone how to do something is sometimes necessary in order to teach him to do it, but it certainly is not sufficient. Many people competent in the techniques of check-writing still do not pay their debts.

b) The second example of ordinary language analysis in education is taken from an article by J. Roland. Roland [11] bases her articles on Ryle's classification of "knowing that"

34

and "knowing how" sentences. She reminds us that Ryle's object in writing *The Concept of Mind,* in which he sets forth the knowing that/knowing how distinction, was to discredit the Cartesian dualism, "the Myth of the Ghost in the Machine;" that, "knowing how" was not a stepchild of theory; and, that all knowing is not "knowing that." Although Ryle's distinction has been criticized as an oversimplification, Roland contends that it is of practical importance to analyze various types of "knowing how" and "knowing that" sentences used in ordinary educational statements even if, in the process, the simplicity of Ryle's dichotomy is lost. For just as Ryle has drawn attention to the dangers to education inherent in the reduction of "knowing how" to "knowing that," one may also point out the dangers involved in a reduction of "knowing that" to "knowing how." It would seem no more desirable to teach mathematical or historical facts as if they were skills like swimming than to teach swimming as if it were Latin or geometry. An equally grave mistake would be to teach moral judgments and rules of conduct as if they were either Latin or swimming. To summarize to this point, Ryle's distinction between "knowing how" and "knowing that" is really a distinction between knowing how to perform skills and knowing statements of a factual nature.

Can all educational sentences regarding knowing be reduced to these two categories? Roland responds negatively, arguing that such sentences as "Johnny knows that he ought to be quiet" and "Jones knows that he should be honest" cannot be reduced to Ryle's classification. To resolve this weakness in Ryle's system of classification, Roland breaks down the "knowing how" category into two types of sentences which she labels Type A and Type B. Type A sentences are those "knowing how" sentences which require practice and which must be demonstrated in an overt manner. Type B sentences are those "knowing how" sentences which can be demonstrated on a verbal level. What Roland and Scheffler are demonstrating is the sorting out of uses of sentences of certain types, attempting to derive paradigmatic cases for analyzing other sentences.

c) Peters' [12] analysis of the term *character* provides us with the third example of ordinary language analysis. Why, one might ask, select any given term over another as an object of analysis? There are no standard criteria for making that selection, but, since it is the ordinary language analyst's self-appointed task to analyze the ordinary uses of any given term or set of terms, a "revival of interest" in the use of a term would make it "ready game" for study. Such is the case with the term *character*. Peters scans the recent history of the word, pointing out that at one time inquiry of several types flourished and then came to a halt, but that, in recent years, character has once again been brought into the spotlight. He finds this sequence to be the same in psychology and sociology, as well as in philosophy. He then asks the standard question, What are the ordinary uses of the word? and finds that these can be classified into three types of use, or what he calls "three ways of speaking." The first of these he calls the non-committal use, by which he refers to our most general use of the term, that is, our use of the term as a way of referring to the sum-total of a man's character-traits. The second class of use is that demonstrated when we use the term *character* in reference to character types. Character, in this sense, is conceived of in terms of a dominance of a single trait—an anal character, for example—or of an exaggeration of a range of traits— parsimonious character, for example. The third way of speaking of character, according to Peters' analysis, is to talk of having character, by which is meant that control and consistency of manner are considered more important than any particular character-trait or set of these. Peters, after completing his sorting out of uses of the term, briefly discusses how the clarification of uses of the term may assist in resolving the problems of moral education.

d) In addition to studying the uses of a particular word because of its frequency of use, one may study the uses of a word because of its current political and social significance, and this is what Komisar and Coombs do in respect to the term *equality*. In their paper,[13] they set forth and try to justify their claim that there are two uses of equality which are frequently confused. These two uses are "equal as same" and "equal as fitting," the first being descriptive and the second being ascriptive. The sameness concept has a determinate definition, while the fittingness concept has an indeterminate definition; that is, its meaning shifts across many contexts and among users. Although there are certain difficulties in clarifying the meaning of the first term, "equal as same," much greater difficulties are encountered in attempting to establish the criteria for definitions of "equal as fitting." What Komisar and Coombs do establish are rules for judging whether or not the term *equal* is being used in the fittingness sense. By talking of equality with terms such as ascriptive, indeterminate, and rules of judgment, Komisar and Coombs are led to conclude that equality is a normative rather than a prescriptive term, with all the problems entailed in that category of terms.

In this section, I have attempted to define and illustrate four types of language analysis used in the clarification and explication of educational concepts. Since the last of these four types, ordinary language analysis, is the most commonly used, I have provided four examples of such analysis. Criticisms of language analysis in general and of the examples given in particular are forthcoming, following a short treatment of steno-language.

Steno-Language

Underlying all four approaches to the analysis of language illustrated in the preceding section was the search for standardized definitions of terms. Best, in his uncovering of the hidden premises in educational psychology, assumed certain standard definitions of is and ought; Mosier proclaimed symbolic logic as a way of standardizing the formal language of instruction; for Ayer, sentences are meaningless unless they conform to the tautological standard or to the standard of empirical verification; and, for our ordinary language analysts, the primary goal was to sort out standard uses of terms which could be formalized as paradigm cases. The term *steno-language,* one adopted from Wheelwright,[14] will be used in this work to refer to all definitions which are established by stipulation, by formal rule, or by ordinary usage. Hence, that which has been discussed to this point in the chapter has been steno-language,[15] the presuppositions of which were set forth in the first chapter. Is steno-language adequate for talking about ordinary experience? In general, the answer is no. But, as Schrader has suggested, "There is no intrinsic reason why linguistic analysis should not enlarge its sphere of meaning to include the whole of existence." [16] The purpose of the critical section which follows is to determine the limits of steno-language for talking of first person experience.

Critique

A critique of the analyses summarized to this point could consist of specific criticisms of each analysis. For example, Best could be criticized for attempting to impose on a domain of practice the logical requirements of pure theory; at the level of ordinary experience, can the "is" be separated from the "ought"? Furthermore, the requirement for sorting out ought sentences is a prior one, necessitated by certain preconceptions of the subject matter of educational psychology. If one accepts neither his definitional requirements of educational psychology nor his theoretical distinction between is and ought sentences, then he cannot hold the "offender" to his claims. Mosier, in his attempt to formulate a standardized language for education from symbolic logic, brings into his argument at the very beginning a value judgment as to what should be emphasized in the instruction-learning equation, and, at no point, does he say how his schema $p \leftrightarrow q$ would work. Symbolic logic is adequate for dealing with a limited range of propositions, primarily those of theoretical nature. But, education is not theoretical; it is first-person experience, and, hence, not amenable to the kind of symbolic structuring proposed by Mosier. Ayer could be criticized, as he has so many times before, for his commitment to the verification principle. Quine,[17] for example, offers excellent arguments to the effect that reference proves itself behaviorally inscrutable. His illustration of attempting to empirically verify the presence of a rabbit is both delightful and illuminating. When we point to a rabbit, are we pointing to the "whole" rabbit, to its parts, or to its movements? His reasoning is sound, but in his quest for exactness of usage, Quine discards reference as a criterion. At the level of ordinary experience, however, we do use reference as a major criterion. If we point to a textbook while lecturing, the students immediately catch the meaning, the intention, and there is no necessity of attempting to catalogue all the sense properties of the book, nor to differentiate between the collocation of sense properties and the noise *book*. At a highly technical level, given certain sets of assumptions and definitions, such distinctions can be made, but, at the level of ordinary experience, such language games are not necessary for either communication or learning. As for the ordinary language analysts, for all their contributions to the clarification of the uses of language, their search for paradigmatic cases as a way of standardizing usage is a naive social empiricism, opposed to creative and novel uses of language. As Polanyi [18] has pointed out, when language, which has no intrinsic meaning, is used by a person in an episode of experience the language is given meaning. In other words, language usage is a rich tapestry of ever growing richness; to formalize usage with paradigm cases is to make sterile the language itself and is to force creative persons and practitioners of education to ignore the philosopher's work. Ordinary use is not necessarily the exemplar of communication.

These specific criticisms could be elaborated on at considerable length, but there are at least two general questions that must be attended to, one having to do with the requirement of exactness and the other having to do with the claim of assumption-freeness. The exactness, or precision, requirement of most language analysts applies to the definitions of terms, either single words or sentences. The definitions may be obtained either from referents or from use, but, regardless of the argument over this point, the requirement for exactness of definition is agreed to. Waismann has directed criticisms of the exactness requirement at both types of definitions.[19] He argues, first of all, in a manner similar to that of Quine, who was referred to earlier, against the possibility of referential exactness, using a cat as his example. In another example, this of the word *friend,* Waismann demonstrates that a word of this type makes the requirement for exactness even more difficult to achieve. The difficulty, says Waismann, is that it is impossible to delimit our definitions of empirical concepts in all possible directions. There is always the possibility that a new particular will appear on the scene which possesses characteristics unlike those called for by definitional concepts. We can delimit concepts in some directions but not all, not as long as there is the possibility of new characteristics, of new comparison criteria, etc. In the case of something such as the auto mechanic's understanding of the relationship between compression ratios and valve functioning, a high degree of exactness is possible, if for no other reason than that the parameters are fairly well known. But the degree of exactness decreases significantly when one begins to speak of human character, as in Peters' attempt, or to understand interpersonal relationships, yet one cannot say that truthful statements about character or interpersonal relationships are any less important and real than statements about internal combustion engines. To make exactness the criterion of truthful, meaningful statements and concepts is to make that which is most human the least truthful, the least meaningful to talk about.

The requirement for exactness also fails to hold for the reason that it cannot meet its own demands. This failure is evident whether one is speaking of referential approaches to language exactness, or of symbolic logic as an ideal language for obtaining this precision, or of the ordinary language analysts' search for paradigmatic cases as a way of establishing exactness of use. The referential approach possesses the same logical problem as the verification theory; it, itself, cannot be empirically verified. The ideal language approach eventuates in either an infinite regress or in the discarding of all experiential terms for which the ideal, exact language is inadequate to handle. And, in the case of ordinary language analysis, the paradigm case is a construct which one does not find in ordinary usage. To sum up this point in the words of Polanyi, "The precision of a word will ultimately always rely, therefore, on a test which is not precise in the same sense as the word is said to be." [20]

Exactness, as a requirement for meaningful use of language, has been criticized on two accounts: one, that to make exactness *the* criterion is to disallow meaningful talk about most of that which is distinctly human; and two, that the requirement itself possesses logical problems of sufficient magnitude to discourage language analysts from making wholesale generalizations of it. Language can never be precise in the sense that it possesses complete objective meaning. In what sense, then, can language be considered exact? Language can be considered exact to the extent that it is understood without a great degree of equivocacy. And, understanding is here used in the sense of communicating, as that term is defined in the following chapter, that is, as one's sense of having-in-common. Exactness, then, is the subjective sense of having a certain meaning in common with others and is not an objective criterion at all.

Assumption-freeness is the second general question to be treated. The assertion for years from analytic philosophers has been that their work was free of assumptions and presuppositions, excepting a few axiomatic ones required by a given symbolic system. Implied in this work, however, has been the contradicting assertion to the effect that analytic philosophy is one with the sociological-nomothetic orientation of Western intellectual history and, therefore, shares the presuppositions which were set forth in the first chapter. Particularly strong among ordinary language analysts has been the claim of assumption-freeness. Peters,[21] for example, claims that all he is doing is helping keep theory straight by analyzing the language and concepts of theory. And Soltis [22] claims that he is not attempting to convert anybody to a particular brand of philosophizing, but, of course, it is that brand, ordinary language analysis, which wins all the arguments in his introductory book for students. What else is the student to think after reading Soltis' book but that Soltis is right? If a particular method of analysis sets forth a certain requirement, such as exactness, the requirement carries with it a set of assumptions regarding the nature of truth and meaningfulness and, perhaps, usefulness. As my students have discovered, when one begins with Ryle's typology of "knowing how" and "knowing that" sentences, certain epistemological assumptions are brought into consideration with the typology. If, as Peters says, the task of analytic philosophy is to keep theory straight, then explanatory theories are presupposed; if explanatory theories are presupposed, then certain assumptions regarding the possibilities of explanation are brought into the picture. The general idea of having no general ideas is rather self-contradictory.

Steno-language and Ordinary Experience

What does this summary and critique of language analysis in education tell us that is relevant to the study of education as ordinary experience? It tells us, first of all, that steno-language cannot provide the conceptual tools for talking about first-person experience in any terms other than emotive, expressive ones. The requirement of standardization of the use of terms prevents it; the demand for public verifiability prevents it; and the insistence on explanatory theories prevents it. With its emphasis on objective standardization of language, steno-language eliminates man from his own speech, treating the latter as if it were a machine independent of man. But, to use the terms of Waismann,[23] I-sentences are the very end points of verification; it is they which establish the connections between sentences and reality. In short, steno-language will allow us to speak of educational institutions, methods, organization, etc., but not of education itself. Steno-language is not the language of ordinary experience and, hence, cannot come to grips with education itself.

In the beginning of the first chapter, the existential paradox was defined as the conflict between two types of sentences, those of Type A pointing toward objective generalizations with those of Type B being limited to the phenomenological perspective of individuals. This chapter has treated of philosophical analysis which admits only sentences of Type A to the domain of meaningfulness. The thesis of this work, however, is that education is first-person experience, and, therefore, philosophizing which is relevant to education must concern itself with sentences of Type B. The following two chapters begin a detailed study of such sentences.

Chapter III

OTHER PRELIMINARIES

Language and Experience

If we are to develop ways of talking about ordinary experience, where do we begin? A radical shift of focus is called for. Instead of starting with a standardized language, with its canon of exactness, which precludes all but the most limited use of terms and sentences stating idiographic, novel, open, and multidimensional experience, let us start with that which is given to us in ordinary experience and work from that, asking what is there in ordinary experience which is sharable, verifiable, mutually observable. In other words, if the language is to be of ordinary experience, then it should begin with its own phenomena, rather than asking of generalizations, categorical statements, rules of observation, etc., to do that which they cannot do. This shift of focus is an important one, for in beginning our inquiry into language at the point of the new focus, the base is being established for a new conception of both explanation and epistemology.

It may be true that what we feel is incorrigible, as has been long argued, but what we do to make sense of that can be corrigible. Even if we accept the conclusion that the incorrigibility of experience prevents our saying what it *is*, this does not prevent our saying what *it is like*. Rather than being put off by the difficulty of talking of experience and declaring it to be a matter that is philosophically inconsequential, we should accept it as being worthy of investigation, for, if ordinary experience is first person experience, then to be true to ourselves as well as to the educational enterprise we must find ways of speaking meaningfully about that which is most genuinely ourselves.

To talk, then, of ordinary experience means that a radical reinterpretation of language must be accomplished. There is already a sense in which language is constantly being reinterpreted and expanded in everyday use. Each use of a particular word is in a slightly novel way. No two parakeets, for example, are the same; hence, each time I use the word *parakeet* in reference to a different one, I am expanding the meaning of the word. This is a perfectly acceptable expansion of the meaning of the word, for it stays within the rules of the biological game. A scholar, on the other hand, may, as a result of his inquiry, bring about a radical reinterpretation of the rules of the game by changing the taxonomy. Assuming we accepted the new taxonomy, from that moment on we would not only use new words, but we would also look for different sets of characteristics in the birds we observe. In effect, we would see the world in a different way.

In changing the biological taxonomy, however, the scholar would simply be transposing one set of standardized terms for another. This is the nature of most scholarly activity. Standardized language makes one's area of inquiry much easier to "hold" and to organize than the conglomerate, chaotic flow of ordinary experience. (*Ergo*, biology is easier than education!) As Langer [1] has pointed out, once thinking in standardized terms begins, it runs on in its own loosely syllogistic pattern from one proposition to another, and where it comes into contact with any material of experience, it puts its seal of fixity, categorical division, etc., on every emerging idea and "automatically makes entities out of any element that will take the stamp of denotative words." If we could devise a consistent way of translating either all aspects of ordinary experience into the language of one sense only or a single aspect into a standardized language, we would then have a set of statements which would be logical and scientific; that is, it would be internally coherent and consistent with the data, but it would be patently false for it would exclude those aspects of experience not translated into the terms of the standardized language. To talk about ordinary experience requires that we talk in new ways.

The optional, simultaneous character of ordinary experience, that is, the constant operations among options—neurological, muscular, eidetic, symbolic—is so complex there is

44

no empirical or mathematical model for it. But this optional character is a "fact" and a "sense" of ordinary experience which may be referred to qualitatively as vitality or *élan*. This vitality suggests the non-categorizability of ordinary experience, for one's experience cannot be sorted out into psychological categories and ontological categories, into categories of fact and categories of value without destroying experience itself. Harries has concluded, in the course of developing another thesis, that originally the world is known in an engaged rather than a detached manner and that on "this rather immediate level of experience we find no clear split between fact and value." [2] The language, then, for this engaged level of experience will have to be made up of simultaneous symbolic units, or, to borrow a tentative definition from McLuhan,

> a collocation, a *parataxis* of components representing insight by carefully established ratios, but without a point of view or linear connection or sequential order.[3]

Or, to borrow an additional, yet still tentative, definition, Langer speaks of gestalt-symbols having "multivalent elements, serving many purposes at once." [4]

But before clarifying these definitions and working from them toward a language of ordinary experience, certain preliminary considerations are necessary. That which was referred to as the optional, simultaneous character of experience needs explication; the question of self-identity needs to be dealt with; and a preliminary definition of communication is called for.

The Field-likeness of Ordinary Experience

Certain of the terms used to this point—gestalt-symbols, simultaneous optionality, and the tentative definition from McLuhan—would seem to indicate a field explanation of ordinary experience. Such, however, is not the intent, for, while the term *field* will be used, it will be used in a special sense rather than in the sense of its use by Köhler and Lewin.

As used by Köhler,[5] the term *field* meant that the neutral processes associated with perceptual facts are located in a continuous medium and that the events in one part of the medium affect other events in a manner dependent on the properties of both. As used by the layman, the term simply refers to a system of interactions, but, in this special sense of Köhler's the term refers to theories that work with a continuously spread medium and use partial differential equations as the symbolic tool for explaining both the nature of the medium and the functions therein. Lewin's use of the term [6] was very similar to that of Köhler's, though he was careful to specify that the events in question were psychological, as opposed to physical and physiological ones. With this distinction made, he could describe the dependence of events in a medium, a field, much in the manner of Köhler. The principal characteristics of Lewin's field-theory are summarized by Hall and Lindzey in the following manner:

> (1) behavior is a function of the field which exists at the time the behavior occurs, (2) analysis begins with the situation as a whole from which are differentiated the component parts, and (3) the concrete person in a concrete situation can be represented mathematically.[7]

Lewin's second principle, that analysis is to begin with the situation as a whole, poses an immediate stumbling block to the analysis of ordinary experience. This emphasis on the whole is not peculiar to Lewin's own field-theory, for it was implied in Köhler's definition and made explicit by Wertheimer, who said that "part-processes are themselves determined by the intrinsic nature of the whole." [8] Again, this emphasis poses an insurmountable problem for the use of field-theory in the explanation of ordinary experience, for two reasons: 1) it is but another nomothetic approach, seeking mathematical laws which will explain all human action; and 2) even if one granted this particular nomothetic approach, knowledge of the whole is the necessary prerequisite, and who can grant that? In our ordinary experience, we simply do not know the outer boundaries of that experience; even in a given moment in an experience about which we could say, "It is a small one," the whole is not known. If it were knowable, it would only be so *after* the experience.

If, on one hand, reductionistic approaches are rejected and, on the other, field-theory's "analysis from the whole" is likewise, what approach is left for talking about ordinary experience? A more modest approach is to begin by admitting that experience cannot be named, either in part or in whole; that is to say, we can never say what experience is, what *it* is. We can only describe certain features of *it* as these are given to us in awareness. The term *modest* was used advisedly, for not only does this approach preclude naming, in both its Aristotelian and language-games senses, but it also denies the possibility of a definitive list of the features of experience to be described. The making of such a list would presuppose knowledge of the whole of experience. What, then, are some of the features of *it* which are given to us in awareness? When we reflect on our experience, we become aware that *it* does not flow in the direction of a linear line, nor does *it* flow in single directions; experience, we find, can only be described as non-linear and multi-dimensional. Alan Watts' discussion of wiggles [9] provides a delightful illustration of the non-linearity and multidimensionality of experience. Watts says that all experience is wiggles but that a long time ago man discovered that he could, for a moment, stop the wiggles of fish with a fishnet. In so doing, man imposed a type of order on chaos. Centuries later, man imposed a fishnet, made of lines on paper, on the world and talked about longitude and latitude, on "mathematical wiggles" and talked about plotting on graph paper, on cities, and talked about street grids. Watts could have carried the matter further by pointing out that when man internalized the fishnet image, he was then able to talk about categories of thought, taxonomies of the world, etc.

But our awareness of experience tells us more. It also tells us that the non-linear, multidimensional features occur simultaneously, that experience is a simultaneous mosaic, a dynamic tapestry, acting at many levels of many meanings at once.

Listen intently to a voice singing without words. It may charm you into crying, force you to dance, fill

47

you with rage, or make you jump for joy. You can't tell where the music ends and the emotions begin, for the whole thing is a kind of music—the voice playing on your nerves as the breath plays the flute. All experience is just that, except that its music has many more dimensions than sound. It vibrates in the dimensions of sight, touch, taste, and smell, and in the intellectual dimension of symbols and words—all evoking and playing upon each other.[10]

Here Watts is attempting to communicate what McLuhan calls the all-at-onceness of experience. Watts is also saying that the individual is one with his experience; it is not a matter of the individual's being set apart from, being an objective observer of, his experience, for, in each episode of experience, the individual is not an individual in any classical sense. You can't tell where the music ends and the emotions begin; you cannot separate experience into component parts without destroying the experience itself. As Wheelwright puts it, "The *I* who am aware of the *that* of which I am aware are but two aspects of a single sure actuality." [11] Hence, we may summarize to this point by saying that not only is ordinary experience non-linear, multidimensional, and simultaneous, it is also non-segmental.

Given such characteristics of experience, are there not overwhelming difficulties in the pursuit of a language for experience? The answer is, yes, there are difficulties, though not overwhelming ones. Most of the difficulties arise from our narrow assumptions regarding the nature of language, the criteria of meaningfulness, etc., which have become so much a part of our intellectual world we tend to see experience through the perceptual blinders of our assumptions about language. McLuhan has stated [12] that in certain earlier periods, seeing life as being configurational and talking of it that way was a very "easy habit." Where were the overwhelming difficulties then? Even now, the Oriental world has no concept of "substance" and "substantial form," since its languages contain no "pressure" to break experience up into analytic units. With the pressure of our language to assign names to what is going on in the world, we do experience difficulty in talking of that for which no names are assignable.

To return now to the original question regarding the adequacy of field-theory for talking about ordinary experience, the conclusion is that, as set forth by Lewin and the Gestalters, field-theory is not adequate but that the language of ordinary experience will have to be "holistic" in some sense. The sense of the term is to be found in the shift away from the naming of experience to an episodic, metaphorical describing of experience; experience is like a field, though not a field.

Self-Identity in a Field of Experience

One of the major difficulties in holistic systems—whether of the type of Lewin, or of the Gestalters, or of social-process theories such as those of George Mead and Dewey, or of Oriental thought, which has provided much of the inspiration for Watts' work—has been that of accounting for the individuality of human persons in the whole. The individual is assigned the status of a part of the larger reality from which he derives his own, but his own reality is never really his own, for, to use the terms of Lewin, he is but a set of regions within a larger set. In respect to individuals, holistic theories have never been able to shake free from Hegelianism to any significant extent. Is it contradictory, then, to say that, in a given episode of experience, I am at one with that experience, and, at the same time, to say that I have identity within that experience? I think not.

There are, at least, three means whereby I can establish my own identity in a field of experience: 1) through a process of counterfacing I can delimit a sector of personal meaning; 2) through my intentional and non-intentional creative use of language I can demonstrate what Wheelwright calls *perspectival individuality;* and, 3) through non-mediated awareness I can know which "side" of the organism/environment paradigm I am on.

Granted that there are no discrete individuals, for even the meaning of 'individual' occurs in a context of conglomerate flow of experience. In this sense, 'individual' is a particular meaning of experience; to focus on a particular meaning, then, without destroying it, one must use a process of counterfacing, a process in which two or more meanings are placed in juxtaposition for determining contrast, simi-

49

larities, and interrelationships; in short, for determining identity. This method of analysis permits one to delimit a sector of meaning without destroying the meaning. In other words, we may become aware of our own experience through a counterfacing with other experience, with what McLuhan calls [13] antienvironments which make us aware of our "normal" environments.

Wheelwright's *perspectival individuality* [14] refers to our using language in such a way as to create new meanings. Unintentionally, we do this in the manner described earlier in the chapter when we use a class word to refer to a new particular; in so doing, we have enriched the meaning of the class word. We may also do this intentionally in our use of everyday language, or we may, also intentionally, do this in the creation of a poetic expression or with new slang phrases. Every such creation of language usage represents a perspective that is individual, in the sense that it is in a class of its own (except in abstract and rather irrelevant ways). Individuality is a characteristic of ordinary experience whether we are aware of it or not, for, as was pointed out, we frequently use language in creative ways unintentionally. It would follow that greater awareness of individuality would result from more intentionality.

Two frequently used terms for denoting the unity of the individual and his field of experience are organism/ environment and convex/concave. The first of these stresses the point that there is no word for that boundary-of-interplay between the organism and the environment as well as the point that there is no inside-outside dichotomy. One may ask, for example, if the hamburger you just ate is inside you, and it can be argued quite cogently that the hamburger is not, in fact, inside you. The point is that the "play" between the organism and the environment knows no distinct boundary. The second term, convex/concave, attempts to express the same matter, using a geometric model rather than a biological-ecological one. But, a point overlooked by those who rely heavily on these two terms is that, at the level of ordinary experience, I am aware, at least in a gross sense, of which is me and which is environment. I do not attempt to put a suit on the environment; I do it, with varying degrees of success, on myself. Although I am aware of the field-likeness of my experience, I am aware at the same time of the part of the organism/environment paradigm to which I can assign the word *me*. Even though I am in and of a field of experience, I am aware of self, not in the sense of absolutizing the ego, but through a nonmediated "knowledge" of which is me. This awareness of self is not a self-concept, in the manner of current social theories, but is of my body as the condition of knowing and intending.

We have seen, from the preceding discussion, that it is meaningful to talk of individuals even while speaking of the field-likeness of experience. Implied in the concept of ordinary experience is the concept of individual. To assert otherwise is to negate the claim that ordinary experience is non-nomothetic.

On Redefining Communication

The term *communication* is usually used in a strictly utilitarian sense, referring to transfer of a message through a process of encoding, mediating, and decoding. Thus, if the message is not "run through" all three parts of the process, communication has not taken place. The effectiveness of communication is directly contingent upon accurate encoding, freedom from distortion in the medium, and accurate decoding. As so used, the process meets its utilitarian criterion, for it is quite effective in disseminating information over a wide spectrum of topics to a wide range of publics. But, since that which is most sharable is the least personal, communication, defined in utilitarian terms, is at best only appropriate for the most superficial levels of experience. If we begin with ordinary experience, which includes both that which is most personal as well as some of that which is public, will it be meaningful to talk of communication? If so, in what sense will the term be used? These are the questions of this section. In constructing answers to these, consideration will be given to the work of Langer on her criticisms of utilitarian theories of language, to Lewin's concept of locomotion as communication, to Borgmann's definition of communication, and to Madden's analysis of isomorphisms.

Langer's criticism of the genetic theory of language [15] consists of arguments to the effect that the theory does not account for the phenomena of art, ritual, magic, and dreams or even for the practical, "realistic" uses of language. The genetic theory is that which holds that language is the latest and highest-device of animal evolution, thus allowing the essential difference between man and other animals. Language's possession of tool-value, for this theory, is its highest good, for this utility value permits man to do practical things not possible for lower animals. Langer first criticizes the theory's claim that it can account for the practical, the "realistic." She provides several examples of human linguistic behavior which are quite impractical, erroneous, distorting, unrealistic, and even disgusting. If language is that evolutionary tool which gives man the power to deal with the world in a more practical and realistic way than can other animals, why does he use it in such impractical and unrealistic ways? Either there is some "force" prior to the language which brings about the misuse, or the conception of language is inadequate to account for such "misuses." These considerations lead to the second criticism, which is that a strictly utilitarian explanation of language, such as that of the genetic theory, will not account for art and ritual, among other phenomena; these are merely play or acting, as, for example, one plays an instrument or acts in a play. They are, in short, superfluous, not necessary utilities. Yet, even in times of war, armies, through either tacit or open agreement, do not destroy works of art. Why? Langer draws her answer from her theory of mind. The human mind, says Langer, is a transformer of experience; as such, transformations will take place in different media and in quite different overt directions, not necessarily in utilitarian ones.

Langer's criticism of utilitarian theories of language is appropriate to the work here, but there are two reasons why her own conception of symbolic transformations does not provide a definition of communication appropriate to ordinary experience. One is that her explanation is grounded in a particular conception of mind which, though not at odds with the concept of ordinary experience, is not especially relevant, in the sense that the concept of ordinary experience need not be grounded in her theory of mind. The second is that Langer's theory is not directed toward the matter of communication, but toward the question of the nature of language itself and its relation to mind. Hence, although Langer's work is helpful at this point and will be referred to on occasion, for a definition of communication appropriate to the purposes of ordinary experience, we must look for other grounds.

Because of the field-likeness of ordinary experience, it would appear that certain insights could be gotten from Lewin's explanation of language as set forth in his field theory.[16] In his theory Lewin treats of communication as locomotion. By 'locomotion' he means the movement from one region in a field to another. If we recall that he is primarily concerned with psychological fields, we can see that he is not speaking necessarily of gross muscle movement, but of the relative accessibility of and movement into one or more regions of another's life space. If all locomotion is communication, an ambiguity never made clear, then to communicate is to literally participate in a part of another's life space. If by 'life space' he meant ordinary experience, Lewin would have provided the necessary definition of communication. But his concept *life space* is intermeshed in a network of assumptions and concepts which would have to be accepted also; neither of the terms *locomotion* or *life space* can be separated from this network, a network of assumptions and concepts rejected earlier in the chapter.

The affinity of ordinary experience and phenomenology would suggest that in the literature of phenomenology one might find possible clues to a definition of communication appropriate to the concept of ordinary experience. An article by Borgmann on language in Heidegger's philosophy [17] does provide one very appropriate clue. He points out that since human existence is essentially being-with-others and since language is a mode of human existence, then language is a form of being-with-others. It follows from this that language is not just communication in a technological, utilitarian sense, but is communication "in the deeper sense of having in common." This "having in common" is the clue. To go beyond Borgmann, this "having in common" [18] is not an economic notion of having in common, but is the sense of communication had when people say: "I dig his message," or "Man, he makes contact," or "I read you loud and clear," or "Man, he gets to ya," or "Yeah, Baby, I'm on your wavelength," or "That grabs me." Or, it may be the sense of "having in common" when people participate in dance, in musical performance, in dramatic presentation, in religious ritual. It may be the sense of "having in common" had by those who share a poem, in the sense of participating in the meanings of a poem, in a coffee house. Is all of this a definition of communication in ordinary experience? Not a definition, but definitely a characterization of the nature of communication in ordinary experience. And, if a definition is to be had, it will have to be one which will be grounded not in a theory of mind or of fields, but in those experiential moments when people have that sense of "having in common."

If the sense of "having in common" is to be the keystone of a definition of communication for ordinary experience, finding the conceptual tools for talking more clearly about this "sense" becomes necessary. Talking about the sense of having-in-common in a way which communicates clearly and which permits a more general treatment can be accomplished by talking about the same phenomenon in different, more rigorous terms, namely, those subsumed under the term *isomorphism*. The concept of isomorphism has been frequently used and analyzed in logical and mathematical circles. In its simplest form, an isomorphism is the series of one-to-one correspondence between the elements of two different sets, where the relationships satisfy a set of axioms.[19] Defined in this manner, the concept would appear on the surface to possess considerable value for talking about sets of psychological events. Attempts have been made, primarily by the Gestalters, to use the concept for this purpose. The two sets to be compared would be the domain of stimulus events, on the one hand, and the domain of sensory events, on the other.

The procedure, according to Madden,[20] of the Gestalters, and others who have attempted to use the concept for explaining psychological events, "was to infer from phenomenological experiences the nature of the correlative physiological process." One of the difficulties in doing this is that, unlike a mathematical set in which the members are known, the set of physiological correlates is pretty much unknown. Because of the lack of factual evidence for the isomorphic assumption and because the assumption cannot, according to Madden's conclusion, be established by logical argument, the Gestalters have been in error in asserting such relationship.[21]

In what sense, then, can the term contribute to an understanding of communication as "having in common?" If we speak of isomorphisms-of-experience, there is no need to claim that all members of any two sets will be in correspondence, and there will also be no necessity for factual knowledge of physiological process. Rather, an isomorphism-of-experience is, in this context, a social-communicative concept, neither a mathematical nor a psychophysical one. It refers to those parallels of experience between and among individuals which make communication of any type possible. True, my experience is mine and mine alone, but this is not to say that I am completely locked inside myself and, thus, cannot have the sense of "having in common" with others. And I can have this communication to the extent that the experience of others parallels mine. When two people are deeply involved in an activity together, communication will take place to its greatest extent, for, although each will have his own experience, the parallels of feelings, muscle involvement, desire, pleasure, fatigue, etc., will be extremely close. When two people have been involved in activities at great physical and psychological distance, communication will be limited to the degree that each can make his experience parallel some similar experience of the other. If there is no similar experience at all, communication, at that point, cannot take place. For these parallels we can use the term isomorphism-of-experience without implying either its mathematical or psychophysical notions. The term is a social-communicative one, referring to the sense of "having in common" between the ordinary experiences of two or more individuals. Communication, defined as isomorphisms-of-experience, is developed at length in the following chapters.

The Language of Ordinary Experience

All preliminary considerations have now been made. In Chapter One, a beginning definition of the concept *ordinary experience* was developed, and the role of that concept in the study of education was established through criticisms

55

of sociological-nomothetic and phenomenological approaches to such study. Chapter Two consisted of descriptions and criticisms of various analyses of the language of education, pointing up their inadequacies for treating of the matter of ordinary experience. And, in this chapter, the concept of *ordinary experience* has been developed in greater detail through discussions of the relationships between experience and language, of the field-likeness of ordinary experience, of the problem of self-identity in a field, and of the meaning of the term *communication*. From these preliminary considerations it has become apparent that the language of ordinary experience will consist of gestalt-symbols, having the power to communicate, as that term has been defined, the simultaneous, idiographic, multidimensionality of experience. The remaining chapters set forth such language and also treat of several related problems, explanation and knowledge being the major ones.

Chapter IV

EXISTENTIAL LANGUAGE

Conceptual Imbalance

According to Kneller,[1] the ordinary language analysts contend that paradox is the resut of conceptual imbalance; this is to say that, when one or more concepts are pushed beyond their limits to the extent that they overshadow the rest, philosophical perplexities and paradoxes result. A philosopher who does this comes to lack a sense of proportion, and his analyses and conclusions suffer from it. But the ordinary language analysts, or informal analysts as Kneller calls them, are guilty of their own contention, for they have focused on paradigm cases of ordinary usage to the exclusion of not only novel uses of language, but to different conceptions of language as well. McLuhan would agree,[2] I think, with Kneller's statement that paradox is the result of conceptual imbalance, but he argues that the imbalance comes from emphasizing one mode of language over others, thereby creating sense-ratios which change men's thinking. As he puts it in an earlier context, "For until literacy deprives language of its multi-dimensional resonance, every word is a poetic word unto itself." [3] What he means by literacy is the emphasis on the printed word and its literal analysis, the *forte* of the sociological-nomothetic orientation. Thus, what would be required for a resolution of conceptual imbalances, of paradoxes, would be a new recognition of the limits of certain concepts and the awareness of our limited constructions of language. When considering the nature of education as first-person experience, this awareness becomes imperative.

Consider the following case. Two groups of university students in an education course decide to communicate to other members of their class the lack of relevance of most current teaching in inner-city schools. One group came to class with a sociological-nomothetic type report; that is, they presented statistics of the situation, socio-economic backgrounds of the teachers in such settings, typical course materials, etc. The class response was typical of university students. They made the appropriate notes and prepared themselves to regurgitate the data on an anticipated test. The second group decided that the factual material could be read from a hand-out but that the real issue was one of communicating in some total sense the agony of students in the inner city who want an education but who find the typical educational offerings completely irrelevant to their lives and to their social situations. The second group, therefore, decided to break away from a presentation using steno-language, though they did not use that term.

Although describing in declarative sentences will not communicate wholly what they did, here is the attempt. When the class came in on the announced day, the room was darkened, and an empty space had been made at the front of the room. A movie projector was ready, as was a record player of high wattage. The movie began. It was an educational film, having to do with the training of dogs, using the techniques of operant conditioning. At the same time two other things happened. The record player began playing softly a currently popular "soul" number, and several students came marching in, in military fashion, behind their "teacher." With no words being spoken, the teacher went through a series of arm motions which the students imitated exactly. At the same time, the relative volumes of sound between the record player and projector were being changed every few seconds. The class began to note that one student in the "statement" was beginning to falter in the group responses to the teacher. This student became more and more agitated, and, at the moment of peak agitation, the sound systems of both projector and record player went full blast, and the student began, first to moan, then to scream, culminating in her jumping up from the group, ripping off her clothes, and running from the room. All the while the "teacher" continued according to his lesson plan, not noticing the girl at all and continuing to train his "dogs." At the end of the film, the students marched forward to the

58

teacher who placed around the neck of each a set of dog tags, and the group marched out in goose step.

A moment of silence followed, and then the classroom was filled with questions. Is it really that bad? Is education really that much out of touch? Are there other factors to which education should attend? Who was right: the ones who remained or the girl who stripped herself of the whole matter and ran out? And the questions ran on and on. The existential language of education had been spoken. The deadening trap of the non-human, sociological-nomothetic language had been broken. For the first time a language had been spoken which communicated not *about* the problems of education, but which communicated the problems of education. Involved in this communication were word modes, and body modes, and pictorial modes, and acoustical modes —all in a simultaneous, gestalt-of-meaning.

Existential language communicates these simultaneous gestalts-of-meaning of ordinary experience by encouraging the use of all bodily expression—all language is a bodying-forth—thereby correcting the conceptual and media imbalances mentioned at the beginning of this section. Practically all of the imbalances have come about as a result of the misuse of written language. In what ways can we broaden our conceptions of written language to make possible the communication of ordinary experience with written language? What is the relationship between the body and language? And, does existential language include more than written language? These are the major questions of this chapter.

The Body and Language

The dominant intellectual tradition of the West has been to make mental categories prior to, and of greater value than, existential happenings. The priority has been couched in many different sets of terms—some philosophical, some religious, some legal, some scientific—but it has rarely been challenged. Resulting from this priority have been such matters as valuing the society over the individual, asserting the reality status of certain rational categories over individual experience, claiming greater value for the "spirit" than for the "physical," and greater value for the intellect than for the animal-body. This dominant priority has taken the form of an assumed bias which permeates Western culture. Certain voices have spoken out against this bias, with Freud being one of the most notable, but the thinking of such as Freud has been negated in various ways, either through direct attack or through dilution of his thought as in the case of the so-called neo-Freudians. And, as pointed out in Chapter One, the sense-empiricist tradition has not changed the priority in respect to the ordinary experience of the individual. The deprecation of the body has remained an implicit goal of the Western intellectual tradition, and philosophy has provided much of the intellectual equipment for the task. As one example, we may note Brown's statement in a chapter titled "The Resurrection of the Body."

> We may therefore entertain the hypothesis that formal logic and the law of contradiction are the rules whereby the mind submits to operate under the general conditions of repression. As with the concept of time, Kant's categories of rationality would then turn out to be the categories of repression.[4]

When the body, which is the origin, ultimate referent, and instrument of all communication is repressed, education is likewise repressed in that it becomes limited to a limited range of language concepts completely cut off from the origins and vitalities of those concepts.

In addition to Brown, who makes his position quite clear in the above quotation, several other writers and philosophers have begun to challenge the implicit bias, though, it must be noted, few, if any, are to be found in philosophy of education. Camus,[5] for example, made the body the basis for all of his earlier thought, and Watts[6] has asserted that one can only know the world in terms of the body. Kaelin[7] has pointed to the obvious, yet overlooked, truth that one's body is always *here*, and that *here* is always the primary reference point of communication. Merleau-Ponty[8] has given extensive attention to the body in communication, arguing that the body is not an object in the world, but, is rather, the necessary condition for knowing the world. One does not perceive his body, except in some mirror image

60

sense, for, to the extent that one does "perceive" his body, he does it with his body. To continue following Carr's explication of Merleau-Ponty, "if expression is taken as 'letting meaning appear,' the perceiving body is already expression *par excellence*." [9]

Psychology, like philosophy, has provided intellectual equipment for supporting the anti-body bias. From introspection to mental states theories to behaviorism the goal has been the same: to find those enduring general laws which would explain human conduct. But, in psychology as in philosophy, there have been, and are, those few thinkers who have recognized the bias and have attempted to counter it. Freud has already been mentioned. More recently, Schutz [10] has argued that "no words are so clear as the language of body expression." And Furth concludes after extensive research on deaf subjects that

The evidence for conceptual thinking of the linguistically deficient deaf leads to the direct conclusion that thinking develops through living contact with the environment regardless of the presence or absence of a ready-made linguistic symbolic system.[11]

It may be claimed by some psychologists that Sheldon, Kretschmer, and Lombroso developed theories grounded in the lived body, but, in response to this claim, it should be pointed out that all three were attempting to impose their conceptual categories onto the body rather than recognizing the body as the source of all language.

In education the same anti-body bias has operated. Physical education, for example, has been able to get its foot in the curriculum door with a healthy-mind-needs-a-healthy-body rationale, an obvious, distorted Platonic derivative. But other bodily expressions—feelings, enthusiasm, etc.— have been suspect in the classroom and, if allowed at all, have been channelled into extra-curricular activities. *The disembodied knowledge of a disembodied language dominates.* One interesting exception to this was the practice of G. Stanley Hall, who, in a course he taught in ethics, devoted the first units of work each term to hygiene and physical education. For Hall,[12] holiness and health is the same word.

61

To turn to a pressing question, what does it do to our conceptions of language to assert that the body is the origin, the ultimate referent, and the instrument of all communication? One might do as McLuhan has done in *Understanding Media* by ignoring the question and talking instead of media as extensions of the body. In that work, McLuhan includes practically every conceivable extension of the body, such as clothing and automobiles, as communication media. Polanyi [13] says, in a footnote, that he would even consider, along with Samuel Butler, Mrs. Bentley's snuff-box as language. Obviously, the assertion regarding the body and language will result in more attention being given to any medium which bodies-forth meaning and less attention to specific formalized languages themselves. This is not to say that no attention will be given to language; it is to say that language loses its meaning when it is analyzed, classified, etc., apart from body origins. Hence, the linguist, the philosopher of language, and the educational media specialist will need to refocus their domains of inquiry and to effect a new balance in their theories. Certain art theorists have already done this. Richards, for example, whose book *Centering in Pottery, Poetry, and the Person* [14] deserves a wider readership, argues at length in a more recent article that all forms are language and that communication flows between all of them, non-verbal and verbal alike.[15] The centering he speaks of is the recognition of body, of body that carries its own referent in movement, and movement in space may take many forms ranging from making pots, to writing poetry, to dancing, to painting, to engineering, to solving geometric problems, to exploring astronomical theory. Richards, writing from his perspective of art theory, has come to recognize that language, conceived of as the bodying-forth of meaning, takes many forms, and that to study language apart from its body origins is to create a domain of inquiry fraught with numerous inhuman consequences. But let us move from this general point regarding the relation of body to language to a consideration of the more specific characteristics of existential language.

Both McLuhan and Watts have frequently pointed out the specializing and fragmenting which results from attempts to speak of simultaneous happenings with written language, and examples have already been given in this work to illustrate some of the difficulties. When we separate things out so that things and events are nouns, actions are verbs, and associated properties are adverbs and adjectives, the result is that things (nouns), which by definition are not action, set in motion that which is action (verbs). We are confronted in speaking of ordinary experience with written language with the fragmentation and specialization which result from the non-action-yielding-action problem, from the difficulties entailed in the general requirement of agreement between subject and predicate, and from the sequential order necessitated by the form of declarative sentences. All of these, which inhere in steno-language, make ordinary language almost totally inadequate for talking of ordinary experience. Watts has suggested,[16] in one reference, that the Nootka model of written language be adopted. The Nootka model drops all nouns and adjectives, using only verbs and adverbs. Hence, a church is "housing religiously" and a store is "housing tradingly." Although the Nootka model may remove some difficulties, it is grounded in a process metaphysic, the claims for which go beyond ordinary experience, and, more importantly, the elimination of adjectives would prevent the metaphorical describing of experience, the claim for which was set forth in Chapter Three. The Nootka model is one attempt to solve the problem, but we must look elsewhere.

Two novelists have made explicit efforts to communicate that which is given in ordinary experience by way of written language. Faulkner, in his *The Sound and the Fury,* attempted to communicate the simultaneous, open field of perception. The term *stream-of-consciousness* is used to refer to his attempt. Since the stream-of-consciousness is not confined to physical space and time, Faulkner had to dismiss most of the rules of grammar, and the non-sequential order within the stream-of-consciousness required that he violate most of the conventional rules of writing. But, with his stream-of-consciousness technique, Faulkner brought us one step closer to an existential language.

A more recent effort by a novelist is that of Julio Cortazar. In his novel *Hopscotch,* Cortazar makes some use of Faulkner's technique, which is now done by many, but goes beyond that to develop another approach to speaking of the simultaneous, non-sequential character of ordinary experience. At the beginning of the book, Cortazar provides the reader with a page of instructions for "getting through" the 155 sections of the novel. In reading the book, however, one actually reads 190 sections, for several sections are read more than once and, each time, in a different order. The reader is forced to give up his conditioned approach to novel reading; that is, he is forced to stop holding onto the threads of the story. He is literally forced to flow from one episode to another, feeling his way along as much as thinking through the work. Cortazar has not set forth an existential language of ordinary experience; he was not attempting to, but he has illustrated that written language can be opened up to account for at least certain aspects the simultaneous, non-sequential nature of ordinary experience.

To leave the work of novelists and return to efforts of philosophers to open up written language, let us look at Wheelwright's concept of plurisigns and Koestenbaum's correlated concept of fringe-facts. The term plurisign is used by Wheelwright to refer to the simultaneous character, the all-at-onceness, of ordinary experience. He defines a plurisign in this manner:

> The power of speaking by indirection and by evoking larger, more universal meanings than the same utterance taken in its literal sense would warrant, is one species of semantic plentitude. But it may also be that the tenor of an image or of a surface statement is not single; the semantic arrow may point in more than one direction. When two such diversely intended meanings are sharply opposed, the result is paradox. But even when the doubleness of meaning is not pushed to the point of contrariety, it may often be the case that more than one meaning is suggested simultaneously by a certain word or phrase or image. Or, more characteristically, there may be a group of

verbal symbols, put together in a certain syntax and suggesting certain images, some more overtly than others, with the result that the interplay of meanings and half-meanings is far more copious than any literal paraphrase could ever formulate.[17]

A plurisign, then, is a multidirectional, simultaneous semantic arrow with many targets (referents), some in much sharper focus than others. Koestenbaum's analysis of what he calls fringe-facts will help clarify the meaning of the term *plurisign*.

According to Koestenbaum,[18] a fringe-fact is an inner event, with experiences, concepts, and modalities such as "space," "time," "consciousness," "being," "synthetic *a priori*," and "psychological necessity" serving as prime examples. His analyses of two statements, one from literature and one from philosophy, will further clarify plurisigns and fringe-facts. His example from literature consists of three lines by E. E. Cummings.

> A. lady through whose profound and fragile lips/ the sweet small clumsy feet of April came/ into the ragged meadow of my soul.

There is a sense in which one may speak of a referential function of these lines. The referents are first love, sexual excitement, and personal encounter. But even denotation depends on a personal coefficient, as Polanyi puts it,[19] and, hence, we must not presume to have exhausted the meaning of these lines merely by listing possible referents. As a plurisign, example A's referents are of a soft focus, intermingled, with indeterminate boundaries, for example A, according to Koestenbaum,

> suggests the complexity, confusion, evasiveness, and indeterminacy of the surging experience of first love ... [it] does not refer to a simple fact, but to something like the sparkling sun on the waves of the water: the vibrancy and vitality of the sparkle disappear when we fix it in a still picture or permanent image.[20]

Note also, that as a plurisign, the meaning is a simultaneous whole, an all-at-once gestalt of experience. Analytic methods fail in dealing with such experiences, for, as Wheelwright put the matter in the quotation above, "the interplay of meanings and half-meanings is far more copious than any literal paraphrase could ever formulate." This impossibility of any literal analysis exhausting the meaning of a plurisign statement of experience may also be expressed in the language of Watts,[21] who says that every definition of a thing or event implies that the event *goes with* a given environment; hence, the *goes with* is a necessary part of the definition.

One additional note should be made at this point regarding example A. Example A is, to use the terms of Koestenbaum, an ego-involved fact as opposed to an ego-detached fact. Steno-language requires ego-detachment, for only with detachment can the demand for public verifiability be met. But experiences are always ego-involved events, and, as such, traditional categories such as between the knower and the known, fact and value, become the constructions of a certain type of language, namely steno-language, and do not reflect the realm of ordinary experience, that realm where education itself occurs. In short, when talking about the language of ordinary experience, no requirement for ego-detachment is made.

Consider Koestenbaum's second example, a statement from Bergson's *Introduction to Metaphysics:*

B.   There is, beneath these sharply cut crystals and this frozen surface (i.e., my perceptions, memories, and habits), a continuous flux which is not comparable to any flux I have ever seen. . . . This inner life may be compared to the unrolling of a coil.[22]

Here is a phenomenological description of the inner sense of time. Example B possesses many of the same features as example A. Example B is, as Koestenbaum puts it, "clearly referential and transcendent, that is, it is a case in which the ego intends a complex, pervasive, and yet clearly present object or fact in experience. The experienced fact is the inner sense of duration." This example shares with example A its complexities, its dependence on gestalt, and its protean characteristics—the evasive, vague, changing, obscure, subtle aspects of experience.

Bergson is telling us, in a highly metaphoric way, how it feels to have perceptions, memories, and habits. In so doing, he accomplishes what particularized analysis cannot. Bergson is using plurisignation rather than particularization, and, in so doing, he accomplishes a different result.

We can now summarize the key features of what have been called plurisigns and fringe-facts.

1. Plurisigns use metaphors for their descriptions; in fact, one may consider different kinds of metaphors as sectors of a given plurisign, sometimes acting singly, though usually woven into a moving idiogram.

2. Plurisigns are protean; that is, they refer to the primary, as well as subsidiary, awareness of the elusive, vague, *élan* of an experience.

3. Plurisigns are always ego-engaged.

4. Plurisigns are gestalten or wholes; they identify the general appearance of experiences, the outline of things, the less obvious facts of experience, the non-habitual, and the linguistically novel.

5. Plurisigns are "internal" rather than "external." "Internal" is used here in a catalytic sense; that is, the plurisign precipitates an image or understanding even though it may not be a part of that being defined. The word is not being used to establish an in-here/out-there dichotomy; that problem has already been dealt with in Chapter Three.

6. Plurisigns are private rather than public in the sense that they are not directly accessible to other people; they are ways of talking about first person experience.

7. Finally, plurisigns, with their metaphorical components, are the only means whereby we can do research on man "from the inside." A first person account of how it feels to live as a human must be stated in such terms; there are no sociological-nomothetic terms adequate for such task.

Metaphors

Metaphors assume such a primary role in the existential language of ordinary experience, explication of their

67

nature and use is required. In fact, given the assumptions regarding ordinary experience as set forth in Chapters One and Three, one may assert that all language of ordinary experience is metaphorical. And the treatment of communication of ordinary experience corroborates the assertion, for the "statements" of experience communicate to the extent that they are metaphorical parallels of experience. Whether one is speaking of synaethesis, an internal integration of sensations from two or more sense-organs, or of "out there" facts, the words, the sentences, the numbers, the movements, etc., are, at best, precise parallels of the experience. To speak of the importance of metaphorical parallels is not to speak non-scientifically. The graph line from a series of readings of a precise laboratory instrument, for example, is not the series of events at all, yet the reasoning about the events—drawing inferences, planning designs for future experiments, etc.—will be done on the basis of the obtained line. As Mumford has pointed out,[23] logically it is just as permissible to conceive of nature metaphorically as it is to conceive of nature as a cunning mechanic who tries to conserve material and to do the job efficiently and with precision. The keenly aware person, whether he be scientist or philosopher or layman, is always conscious of the metaphorical nature of his language. But our concern here is not with the metaphorical status of scientific statements; rather, our concern here is with the nature of metaphor itself and with the use of metaphor in communicating that which is ours in ordinary experience.

Although several different schemes have been devised for classifying metaphors, such as those by Barfield [24] and Wegener,[25] the analysis of Wheelwright is most consistent with the emphasis of this work. Wheelwright [26] differentiates two types of metaphor, the epiphor and diaphor, each representing one of the two functions implied in the term *metaphor* itself. Implicit in the term is the concept of semantic motion, a motion which includes the imaginative act of outreaching and extension of meaning, on the one hand, and the act of creation of new meaning through juxtaposition and synthesis, on the other. The epiphoric metaphor begins with a literal base and then brings about a transference of meaning to something less literal; this is metaphor in the conventional Aristotelian sense. Of epiphoric metaphor, Wheelwright says,

> Epiphoric metaphor starts by assuming a usual meaning for a word; it then applies this word to something else on the basis of, and in order to indicate, a comparison with what is familiar. The semantic "movement" *(phora)* here is characteristically from a more concrete and readily graspable image "over on to" *(epi)* what is perhaps vaguer, more problematic, or more strange.[27]

The epiphoric metaphor, to go beyond Wheelwright, is the sector of a plurisign which approximates more closely than any other that which has been called steno-language. It may, in certain contexts, function in a relatively precise, referential manner, as when a chemist translates his observations into the terms of his periodic table or as when the psychologist states his observations in terms more familiar to him, namely, those of statistics. But the epiphor is not limited to such cases, for synaethesis can add to the vitality of the metaphor by exciting the reader to reflection along two or more sense-avenues at the same time. Unlike stenolanguage, the epiphor permits the expression of the simultaneous nature of experience.

When Koestenbaum discussed Bergson's comment, he states that the comment was both referential and transcendent. By transcendent he means that in ordinary experience and in the language about ordinary experience we create new meanings, meanings for which there are frequently no referents other than the language-experience-gestalt at that moment. Kaelin [28] has insisted that we must recognize an operation of signifying in which the expressed does not exist outside of the expression itself. This creation of meaning in a moment of experience, this creating of an expression which does not refer outside itself, is what Wheelwright calls a diaphoric metaphor. "Hence," he says, "the 'movement' *(phora)* is 'through' *(dia)* certain particulars of experience (actual or imagined) in a fresh way, producing new meaning by juxtapositioning alone." [29] The purest diaphor is probably to be found in nonimitative

69

music, in most abstract painting, and in the plays of certain of the absurdist playwrights. But, without getting involved, at this point, in a discussion of music, painting, or drama for an example of diaphoric metaphor, we can use a very simple one which Wheelwright took from a leftist magazine of the thirties.

> My country 'tis of thee
> Sweet land of liberty
> Higgledy-piggledy my black hen.

Ignoring questions of worth and taste, note that the anti-patriotic meaning is not to be found in any reductionistic analysis of the three lines; rather, the combination of lines, the gestalt of words, literally forces the creation of meaning. There is nothing at all unpatriotic about either the first pair of lines or the third line; it is in the juxtaposition that new meaning is created.

The diaphoric element in the language of ordinary experience allows us to speak of the indeterminate boundaries of possibility, of new meanings and significances to our lives as we form new combinations, new gestalts of experiences, of sensations, of feelings. It allows us to transcend the moment, not by negating the moment, but by creating new meaning in the moment. And that, I think, is what education is all about.

It should be obvious by now that I am not using metaphor in any sort of junior high school fashion; that is, of using metaphor as a way of talking about the unknown in terms of the known. Nor am I using metaphor in the manner of one of the leading spokesmen for a certain type of language analysis in education; that is, using metaphor as simple analogy. That spokesman, Scheffler,[30] first asserts that a metaphor is an invitation to search for an analogy; after making this distinction, he proceeds to use the two terms interchangeably; he then criticizes metaphors in the language of education because they do not meet the criteria he assumes for analogies. No, metaphor is not being used in this way. It is being used here in both its epiphoric and diaphoric expressions as primary sectors of plurisigns.

One additional critical note is to be made, this directed toward Wheelwright and Koestenbaum. Both Wheelwright, with his concept *plurisign* and his analysis of metaphor, and Koestenbaum, with his concept *fringe-fact,* have concerned themselves entirely with written language. They have attempted to broaden the bounds of that which might be called meaningful language, and, to the extent that they have done that, their contribution to an existential language of ordinary experience is major. But there are many aspects of experience which simply cannot be translated into written language, aspects which are frequently the most personal, the most "real," the most genuinely what we are in any given episode of experience. Are these aspects beyond communication? If the answer is no, then education itself cannot be talked about. The answer can be "yes," however, if the focus is shifted from written language to the origin of all expression, namely, the body, for all communication is the bodying-forth of meaning. As Kaelin, citing Merleau-Ponty, has put it succinctly, "In the beginning there is no word, but there is bodily expression." [31]

Non-Verbal Metaphors

Non-verbal metaphors include all body movements and body extensions which intend meaning. That non-verbal expressions communicate more than is possible for verbal means only has been asserted and argued from the first pages of this work, but two additional examples will refocus the matter for the purposes of this section. One of the examples come from Watts in his differentiation of the word *kiss* from an actual kiss.[32] To give someone a kiss is not to write the word on a piece of paper and hand it to him. The touch of lips and tongues, the mutual pressures, and the intermingled smells communicate experiential "data" which are simply not translatable into words, especially the objective, precise words of steno-language. This communication along several sense avenues at once in ways which cannot be translated into other senses accounts in part, I think, for the current interest in encounter groups, new conceptions of multi-sensuous knowing, and in much of what is now referred to as the "new theatre." The second example comes from McLuhan's distinction between the words American flag and the flag itself.[33] The words, flashed on a screen in front of an audience, will not elicit the gestalt

71

of feelings, perceptions, and responses which one associates with the flag itself. A picture of the flag would be better, but the flag itself, a cut of sewn cloth being flapped by the wind and, in turn, flapping the wind, is the gestalt-symbol required for total response.

These two examples do not, however, exhaust the list at all. Other obvious examples are the dance, acting, painting, new uses of film, costuming and gesturing in conversation and song. A special warning is appropriate at this point: the layman, be he teacher or student, may be "put off" by talk of dance, acting, and painting, for, to him, these may communicate "fine arts" or "culture," things which to him are cut off from the everyday world of his experience. No "culture" apartness is being asserted here; in fact, just the opposite is being claimed. Developed into disciplines of their own they are not part of the everyday experience of the layman, true, but the layman does costume himself in certain ways; he gestures in a variety of ways; and he moves about in several fashions. In so doing he is saying something to others about himself and his world. McLuhan, in expanding on his thesis that all media are extensions of the body, says that "All media are active metaphors in their power to translate experience into new forms." [34] The layman, therefore, should be aware that he is already communicating in ways other than his everyday speech and writing and that, in so doing, he is communicating additional, and sometimes contradictory, messages. Basic to all non-verbal metaphors is the gesture, and the layman gesticulates freely. The layman understands this so long as the gesture is conceived of as an explicit symbol, that is, as an act which points to, intends, some object in the world. But the gesture not only has meaning in the sense that it intends some object in the world, it also *is* meaning in that it brings into the world an expression which is the individual nature of the user. Gestures, then, are a part of the vocabulary of even the layman who knows nothing of the so-called fine arts.

Non-verbal metaphors, we may conclude from the above, are major components of meaningful language and as "natural" to every man as is his body.

But are they metaphors? Recall that the "movement" of an epiphoric metaphor is from a more concrete and readily graspable image over to what is vaguer and more problematical. Also recall that the "movement" of the diaphoric metaphor is within the language-experience-gestalt of the moment, creating new meaning in the moment. These two "movements" of metaphor closely parallel the two meanings of gesture given above. In the first of these, gesture possesses meaning in the sense that it intends some object in the world; the object may be quite vague, imprecise, even problematical. Gesture, in this first sense, functions as an epiphoric metaphor. In the second sense, gesture is a meaning in that it brings into the communication an expression new and individual, an expression, as Kaelin puts it, which does not signify anything beyond the expression itself. Gesture, in this second sense, functions as a diaphoric metaphor. Yes, gestures are metaphors, as are all non-verbal expressions, of which gesture is the prototype.

But let us sharpen the focus of the discussion by looking at three specific types of non-verbal metaphors: body metaphors, visual metaphors, and musical metaphors. In the largest sense, all metaphors are body metaphors since all communications are the bodying-forth of meaning. One can differentiate among these on the basis of product, as Dewey has done in his distinction between body-arts and material-arts,[35] but the concern here is not with the product, but with the bodying-forth. The concern with the bodying-forth rather than product, however, will not permit an extremely clean-cut distinction, for, for good singers, singing is a total body activity, to give only one example. In talking of body, visual, and musical metaphors, I am actually talking of only one matter, that of the bodying-forth of meaning. The distinction is made on the basis of the degree of gross muscle involvement required and the requirement for non-organic extensions of the body. Even these two criteria do not permit completely exclusive categories, but they do allow a sharpened focus on each without any claims being made regarding the boundaries of exclusion of each.

Dance and acting are perhaps the two most obvious body metaphors, though a strong case could be made for claiming that sports constitute the most obvious example. The diaphoric function of dance-communication would be generally accepted, I think. Through dance one may express his sense of life's rhythms, his sense of space, and his world as experienced and imagined. Even the person opposed to dance would agree that there is some sort of release, of self expression through dance. He probably would not agree that new meanings are generated in the moment of dance both for the dancer and for the observers. That the dance can also function epiphorically he would also deny. How can dance movements, which have no standardized meanings, tell me anything about the world? A ritual dance he might consider superfluous but understandable since the movements are somewhat standardized. The work of Sharon Chaiklin,[36] however, demonstrates that the very non-standardized movements of some psychotics bring them back into communication with the "objective" world. McLuhan [37] cites the case of American soldiers using dance, of a very non-professional caliber, as a way of effectively counteracting brainwashing attempts. And, Daniel Jordan [38] reports that, in his research on dance, he has been able to communicate certain of Jung's very complex, very abstract themes by way of dance.[39]

Body metaphors, thus, can function as epiphoric as well as diaphoric metaphors, but usually they function as both in mixed ratios. As an example, a university senior met with a small group of students to communicate with existential language about himself and his world. He first formed the group into a circle and then, in the center, placed a water-tight box. In a large silver bowl was blue water. Without any words or music, he poured the water from the bowl into the box, knelt before the box, and, then, made finger-tip contact with each member of the group, each time wetting his finger-tips with water. After completing that, he carried the silver bowl around the group, holding it momentarily over the head of each. When he had finished, the members of the group became aware of the bind they were in. On one hand, they could speak freely of what had been "said." They asked him if he were a competition swimmer. He was. They asked him about the trophies he had won. There were many. These aspects of the communication could be translated with ease into spoken language. But, then, the bind became acute, for they wanted to talk of the intense commitment they "read" in the message; they wanted to talk of the totality of his involvement which they had "read" in the message, but they could not. Finally, one student blurted out that swimming was, for the communicator, his religion. From that point on the communication was discussed in the mythic and metaphorical terms of religion. And that was the nearest approximation they could make to steno-language. The senior had communicated existentially, and the meaning transcended the limits of steno-language. In communicating existentially, his body metaphors had functioned in both epiphoric and diaphoric ways.

In another case, a junior girl, who was quite involved with the black power movement, though she was white, danced, before the class, to The Impressions' "We're A Winner," the song which was, for a while, the theme song of the black power movement. Her dance was total, sensual, a complete merger of body and music. When she finished, the class was hushed. At first, they had been caught up in the rhythm of the music, then in the sensuality of the dance, and, then, as the dance and the music became one, they went beyond response to rhythm and sex to the total, existential message. Later comments confirmed that they saw her complete and unequivocal commitment to the movement and "read" it in a much more meaningful way than had she merely told them of her involvement verbally. These are two examples of communications using body metaphors.

When one speaks of visual metaphors, he speaks of a domain which has received much more attention from philosophers than has the domain of body metaphors. In a dance, the movements are once-for-all, gone, and not repeatable in exactly the same way. In art, on the other hand, there is a non-organic extension of the body which is a product, and, as a product, may be subjected to repeated analyses. This philosophers have done, asking such questions as "Is art a language?" "What, if anything, is communicated by art?" "Is art metaphor?" "What is good art?" "What is a good visual metaphor?" Certain of these questions are relevant here to identifying that which may be called existential language. The questions regarding the language-status of art, the metaphor-status of art, and the nature of that which is communicated in art must be dealt with. Questions such as "What is art?" and "What is good art?", while extremely important, are not relevant to the purposes of this work and will, therefore, not be discussed.

Dewey,[40] antedating McLuhan on the point, asserted that art is not only *a* language, but that each art has its own medium, and, thus, art is many languages. Furthermore, each medium says something that cannot be stated as well or as completely in another medium. Twenty-two years later, Gombrich [41] stated that all the evidence points to the conclusion that the phrase "the language of art" is, in some sense, a meaningful term; at a minimum, it is "more than a loose metaphor." The point is simply that throughout this century certain philosophers have recognized that art is more than mere self-expression, that art, in some manner, actually communicates.

One such philosopher is Aldrich.[42] In an analysis of the types and functions of visual metaphor, he first treats of certain questions regarding the nature of metaphors and how these can occur outside of written language. Following a rather detailed treatment of these questions, he concludes by distinguishing between two types of visual metaphor, types which approximate Wheelwright's categories of written metaphors. Aldrich distinguishes between simile (A is like B) and metaphor (seeing anything-A as anything-else-B produces meaning C). He uses the term *simile* in the same sense of Wheelwright's term *epiphor* and the term *metaphor* in the sense of Wheelwright's term *diaphor*. Hence, one may conclude that what is true regarding written metaphors of the epiphoric and diaphoric types and of body metaphors of the same types is also true of visual metaphors. Visual metaphors communicate either by producing parallels between the experience of the artist and our own experience or by creating new meanings, in the manner of a diaphor, by use of the media themselves.

Aldrich,[43] in another reference, criticizes Mothersill's conclusion that art cannot communicate information. Mothersill [44] had concluded that nothing can be asserted or denied in the language of art. "A picture is at best analogous to a predicate." [45] She said that art can communicate information but only as a supplement to a written language, and, further, no one can learn the language of art unless he first knows the conventions of an ordinary language. Art, then, for Mothersill, is always a secondary, dependent language. At the beginning of the article, she claims that art is a language, but, by the end, art is admitted as a language only on a peripheral, secondary basis. And, as stated, Aldrich criticizes her conclusions; he says that art can be informative and offers arguments to support his contention, but then he backs away from the full implications of his contention by stating that the information communicated is that of an expressive sort rather than that of description. But, if art is visual metaphor in epiphoric and diaphoric ways, then art may be descriptive of one's ordinary experience. When a student hands me a painting or a collage and says, "This is a statement of me," he is not merely expressing emotion; he is saying something actual about his world. He is describing the world as he sees it and the "out-there" world as it affects him.

When one speaks of musical metaphor, he speaks of what is probably our nearest approximation to a pure diaphor, for it is sound; it refers to nothing beyond itself; and, it is rhythmic. Sound has not been previously mentioned in connection with the diaphor, but the connection is an important one, for, in sound, a total, immediate, acoustical environment is given which elicits not just cognitive responses, not just referential responses, but an all-encompassing, total organismic response. It is for this reason that music has been declared as being the highest art or the lowest art, depending on the predispositions, frequently moralistic rather than aesthetic, of the perceiver. The highly repressed, non-self-accepting individual is likely to praise music which he associates with religious or patriotic themes or music which is primarily cerebral, such as certain electronic music, but is also likely to condemn music with strong rhythmic emphasis as being corrupt or primitive. What such a person is testifying to, though he is unaware of his testimony, is that music does elicit a total organismic response. He attempts to deny this by "hemming in" the "meaning" with certain conceptual categories. What he cannot deny, however, is that the connections of cerebral tissues with the ear constitute a larger part of the brain than those of other senses, that the excitation is not just of the ear but is of the total skin surface, that such excitation is non-mediated, and, as Dewey puts it, "sound has more reverberations and resonances than any other sense." [46] That sound is a total environmental massage, eliciting a total organismic response and producing new experience and meaning in the moment of its happening is an accepted fact among the younger generation with its "mind-blowing" music and its discotheques.

But a musical metaphor consists of more than just sound; it also is characterized by rhythm. No claim is being made to the effect that music necessarily entails rhythm, for, logically, one can conceive of one without the other. For the purposes here, it is enough to merely note that the typical case of music includes rhythm. When I speak of rhythm, however, I am speaking of something even more inclusive than music; I am speaking of rhythm as the "ambience of existence," as Doris Humphrey [47] calls it. She elaborates on this "ambience of existence" by comparing it to the water in which a fish moves. The water and the fish have "rhythmical differentials" of which they are probably unaware. She speaks of rhythm as being the "greatest organizer." Is she making rhythm into an ontological category? Perhaps. But that is not our concern here. The concern here is with rhythm as a component in the communication of ordinary experience. If ordinary experience is characterized by rhythmical differentials, which I think it is, then rhythm, whether in music or body metaphors, becomes an important part of communication, when that is defined as isomorphisms-of-experience. It is important to note, at this point, that, although the term rhythmical differentials sounds mathematical, in a complex medium, such as the dance or acting, there are no terms in steno-language for denoting these differentials; rather, the choreographer or the director says, Do it *like* this.

The language-experience-gestalt of the moment, which is the diaphoric metaphor, includes total organismic response and awareness of, and participation in, rhythmical differentials, but, to be a diaphor, the gestalt must also be "self-referential;" it must refer to nothing beyond itself, for the meaning is created within and by the gestalt. Music not only meets the requirement of sound and rhythm, but also meets this last requirement of the diaphor. Watts [48] has said that music is our nearest approximation of Boehme's "sensual language," for it is an end in itself, not referring to anything beyond itself. As Watts puts it in a manner extremely consistent with this work on ordinary

78

experience, "Ordinary language refers to life, but music is living." [49]

Existential Language

Existential language, to summarize to this point, consists of multi-media, gestalt-symbols, finding its corrective to conceptual imbalance in the experiencing-body. The gestalt-symbols are, in their largest sense, plurisigns which may be sectored off into more graspable units-of-understanding with metaphors. And, metaphors, defined as epiphors and diaphors, have been explored in their written and non-written modes. Thus, the presupposition of Chapter One regarding metaphors, namely, that the "logic" of ordinary experience is that of metaphorical parallelism, has reached its point of development.

At the beginning of this chapter, an example was given of a student attempt to communicate the plight of the inner city with the tools of existential language. The chapter closes with another example, this of communicating existentially Camus' abstract isolation-involvement paradigm. The setting for this communication consisted of two classrooms with a passage joining the two rooms. At the door of the first room was the mouth of a tunnel. Into this crawled each subject, including the professor. The tunnel was of rather complex design, low enough to force one to continue crawling, with wet leaves and pieces of fur scattered on the bottom and with no sound save that of an occasional groan or scream coming from a prepared tape. As each of us came out of the tunnel into the second room, we were bombarded by a multitude of sights, lights, and sounds of a psychedelic light and sound show. We wandered about in this until all had come from the tunnel, and, while wandering about, we were drawn into constant conversation, dance, and caress by the students who were "producing" the communication. After all had completed the tunnel trip, a large sheet was placed over us, and we were massaged into one organism by sounds, smells, lights, touches, and our own collective body-heat and breathing.

A discussion period followed, and it was difficult, for individual subjects were grappling with conflicting and

79

extremely personal feelings. Finally, they were able to articulate certain of their feelings. In short, they did not like either. Being completely cut off from others was too much, terrifying, in fact, to some, while the total involvement of the second room completely denied them their own identity. Either extreme was bad, they concluded; some sort of tension between the two had to be found. In forty minutes they had come to an understanding of Camus' paradigm, a multi-sensuous, cognitive/emotive, somatic understanding. And, they had come to understand the paradigm on the same basis that led Camus to assert it.

PART TWO

Chapter V

KNOWLEDGE AND KNOWING [1]

Introduction

A primary goal of philosophy is to be rational, to provide grounds of reason for its assertions; a primary goal of psychology is to be scientific, to provide empirical and experimental grounds for its conclusions. In respect to the questions of knowledge and knowing, both, in pursuit of their respective goals, have tended to ignore a major component of ordinary experience, namely, that of feeling. Education, unlike philosophy and psychology, has no *a priori* commitment to be rational or to be scientific, but, rather, has as its primary activity involvement with developing human beings. Education is committed, therefore, by the nature of this involvement, to concerning itself with the problem of feeling and its relation to knowledge and knowing.

When one surveys representative works in epistemology, such as those by C. I. Lewis, Malcolm, Russell, Ayer, Hintikka, Woozley, and Scheffler,[2] he will observe that the matter of feeling has been either completely ignored or summarily dismissed. Given the usual assumptions about the objective nature of knowledge, it quickly follows that feeling, which is personal and subjective, has no claim to consideration in epistemology. Or, if some claim is granted, feeling is dismissed on the grounds that philosophic method cannot deal with such. A. J. Ayer,[3] for example, is perfectly happy to give the problem of feeling to the psychologists. But, as we shall see, the psychologists have not wanted the problem either. Typical of positions taken in works of philosophy of education in respect to the relation of feeling to knowledge is that illustrated by Scheffler's statement that teaching connotes an initiation into the rational life, "a life in which the critical quest for reasons is a dominate and integrating motive." [4] Throughout the literature of philosophy of education is to be found the same neglect of the topic as is found in the literature of general philosophy. It is not that the category *feeling* is attacked by anyone; it is simply that feeling has been generally held to be irrelevant to the question of knowledge—totally irrelevant when considering the "what" of objective epistemologies, only incidentally relevant when considering the "how" of learning theories.

In its "pre-scientific era," psychology had no qualms about dealing with such common sense notions as feeling; as an example, Dewey, in his *Psychology*,[5] devoted seven chapters to the matter of feeling alone. Later, however, those topics which did not lend themselves readily to experimentation were dropped from the books of psychology. There were, of course, numerous explanations of feeling and emotion. The James-Lange theory was one; the instinct theory of McDougall another. But the only explanation which was allowed was some type of drive-conflict theory, which was supposedly scientific. As Arnold [6] has pointed out, as long as psychologists saw emotion as merely a disturber of the peace, they were not particularly interested in pursuing investigations into the matter.

Notable exceptions to all of the above, however, are the recent work of Arnstine and an epistemological paradigm derived from the thought of Albert Camus. This chapter, then, will summarize certain of the key features of conventional epistemology from philosophy and of learning theory from psychology, pointing to the fact, already indicated, of the inability and unwillingness of both to consider seriously the place of feeling in knowledge and knowing. The conclusion, that the difficulty is a matter of being trapped in steno-language, is to be anticipated by the reader. Arnstine,[7] who has given serious attention to the problem will be, in kind, seriously attended to, but the work of Camus and the paradigm derived from that work will be given primary attention for reasons spelled out in due course.

Philosophy and Knowledge

Given the assumptions of steno-language, the most general question of epistemology becomes quickly answerable:

knowledge is objective and independent of individual human experience. All that remains to be worked out from this is whether or not knowledge is "contained" in Universal Mind, related to mind in some sense at all, at one with Natural Law, a network of symbol-media between the perceiver and the thing itself, or the sum of results of scientific operations. In either case, knowledge is held to be rational itself or, at least, the result of inquiry directed by rationality and free of the protean characteristics of individual feeling. Peirce, for example, in speaking of knowledge of the real, says that "we may define the real as that whose characters are independent of what anybody may think them to be." [8] In other words, knowledge of the real, as with knowledge of anything else, is independent of what any individual person may think, for, for Peirce, knowledge is the effects obtained through certain operations by many investigators.[9] Furthermore, the effects must be observable ones, thereby excluding singular, idiographic effects of ordinary experience. Hintikka [10] gets even further from ordinary experience in his theory of knowledge, asserting that his epistemology is only appropriate for a "world of perfect logicians." Whether he claims to be such or not is not indicated. And Goldman,[11] writing in a similar vein, says that, for his theory to hold, he cannot start from the content of his own experience. Goldman, along with most epistemologists, attempts to sever the language of his theory from his own body, from his own experience, to codify the rules of a rational dialectic which will inform him of the world. As a result of this type of endeavor, philosophy has set forth conceptions of knowledge which are so cut off from ordinary experience, only perfect logicians can understand the theories, and this is asserted with a perfectly straight face. Even the delightful, human characteristic of humor is lost. Disembodied epistemologies are bound to yield conceptions of knowledge which are severed from all that is human with one exception, namely, the ability to completely cut theory off from the ordinary experience of the individual. *And the exploitation of this one exception has made epistemology almost completely irrelevant to distinctly human involvements such as education.*

For many years philosophers of education attempted to find implications for educational theory and practice in various epistemologies. If, for example, it is held that knowledge is "contained" in Universal Mind, then the task of the philosopher of education is to first determine the nature of individual mind and, second, to find the means for bringing the knowledge had by the individual mind into coherence with the knowledge "contained" in Universal Mind. If it is held that knowledge is one with Natural Law, then the task of the educator is to expose his students to natural phenomena as a way of getting the students to "see through" the actual to the essential orderings and structures of Nature. If it is held that knowledge is the sum of the effects obtained through experimental operations, then the task becomes one of developing an experimental pedagogy consistent with pragmatic epistemology. These three assumptions with their corresponding approaches have been described and labeled variously, but a typical shorthand refers to them as the theory that knowledge is received, the theory that knowledge is discovered, and the theory that knowledge is constructed.[12] Although a few philosophers of education continue inquiry along these lines, such work is not now very fashionable. The logical inadequacies of the implications have been quite thoroughly demonstrated, and attempts to experimentally check-out the claimed means have proven inconclusive. But few have seen that to negate the inquiry on logical and experimental grounds is simply to continue playing the sociological-nomothetic game. Not being aware of this point, there is much wringing of hands among philosophers of education with the correlated lamentation that epistemology has little, if any, contribution to make to education. There has been in recent years, therefore, less attention given to the question of knowledge itself and more attention given to analyses of the various processes entailed in coming to know; thus, educational psychology has come to have predominant weight in educational research and in teacher education.

Psychology and Knowing

When the man-on-the-street, including our typical teacher, wishes to say something about human action which he cannot immediately attribute to obvious environmental or historical factors, he will speak of psychology: "Oh,

86

that's psychological, you know." With sentences of this type he intends to refer to the subjective, feeling components of individual experience. But, when one looks to the works of psychologists themselves, especially those who have researched and theorized about learning, he finds that psychology, like philosophy, has little, if anything, to say regarding ordinary experience, for psychology is also searching for those explanatory constructs which are objective and independent of individual experience.

The search has assumed a nomothetic posture, seeking those most general statements of human behavior under which specific cases could be subsumed, hoping to be able to couch statements in terms as quantitative and rational as possible, hence, eliminating from consideration the protean, subjective feeling, idiographic aspects of ordinary experience. Pavlov, for example, is credited with "discovering" the conditioned reflex and with determining the empirical relationships and basic parameters between the reflex, its conditioning variables, and its physiological correlates. For what purpose? To make the psychology of learning into a physiological science, into a domain entirely explicable in terms of certain objective, independent statements or laws. Thorndike, likewise, was searching for laws which would account for all human learning. And he claimed to have found them, though he did modify the claim after 1930. Skinner, who officially is opposed to theory construction, nevertheless asserts that learning can be accounted for by way of the various reinforcement schedules of his operant conditioning. And Hull would explain all learning with his mathematical postulates. These theories will be discussed in detail in the following chapter on explanation, but the point here is, to repeat, that psychology, like philosophy, has eliminated from its considerations the protean, subjective aspects of ordinary experience.

Even though psychology has eliminated such first-person matters from its theories of learning, much has still been written about the implications for education of the theories, with the exception of Hull's mathematico-deductive one. Implications claimed from Thorndike's theory have included the concept of readiness, certain practices of reward and punishment, instructional materials incorporating trial-and-error and drill notions, the importance of studying the part before the whole, and the de-emphasis on such teaching concepts as formal discipline and understanding. In his day Thorndike's influence on educational practice was quite extensive but has now, of course, waned. In the psychology of learning, it is now the influence of Skinner which has come to the fore. Skinner's operant conditioning, though quite technical in its formal statement, has been proven easily adaptable to classroom operations, especially so with the use of programmed instructional devices. Even without the devices, however, the teacher can "program" his material in such a manner as to elicit correct responses immediately, and reinforcement, which may be defined loosely as any attention, can be given those correct responses on the spot. The dramatic success with operant conditioning in the teaching of certain types of subject matter has led to extreme enthusiasm on the part of many school practitioners. But the question at this point is, does Skinner's explanation of learning take into account the first-person aspects of the experience of education? And the answer is no. His "empty organism" postulate, his emphasis on external reinforcement, and his conception of subject matter—all exclude any consideration of first person, subjective experience.

Certain philosophers of education, particularly ordinary language analysts, as a result of their disenchantment with the search for implications, both from epistemology and learning theory, have shifted their focus to the concepts used in talking about the many processes entailed in learning. Among terms analyzed have been overachievement and underachievement, readiness, perception, conception, thinking, learning and teaching, and learning theory itself. (Examples of this type of analysis were given in Chapter Two.) While such analyses have clarified the many uses of these and similar terms, they have contributed little of value to the practitioner of education, and the notion of education as first-person experience has not been considered, by them, to be a meaningful term. Both epistemology and learning theory are consistent, historically and logically, with education defined in sociological-nomothetic terms; hence, both have provided the rationales and designs for much research in learning and curriculum theory. But both, with few exceptions, have ignored the personal coefficient in knowledge and in coming to know.

The Feeling/Notion Paradigm

Given the assumptions of ordinary experience with its corollary of education defined as first-person experience, how can we talk of knowledge and of coming to know? Or should we say that all such talk is irrelevant to individual human experience? Arnstine, grappling with the problem—though it must be made clear that he was in no way consciously working with the concept of ordinary experience, only the problem as he had come to it in his experience—seems to think that we should drop consideration of epistemology as the grounds and guides for education and look to aesthetics instead. It would appear that with his emphasis on aesthetics, on affectivity, on feeling, he might provide significant clues for ways of talking about knowledge and coming to know from the perspective of ordinary experience. Let us see.

Arnstine,[13] early in his work, rejects the approaches which contend that education is either an art or a science. He points out that those who have held that education is an art often conceive of the acquisition of knowledge as an almost mystical union between student and teacher, with terms such as intuition and insight used frequently, and that those who have held that education is a science have tended to put their faith in the collection and dissemination of quantifiable data. He also rejects the approach of those whose primary preoccupation is with language analysis.[14] To merely clarify what is already the case will not resolve the art/science problem nor will it answer the question of feeling in its relation to knowledge and knowing. What, then, does Arnstine propose?

He sets out to provide reasonable grounds for educational practice which will be guided by, and at all points be in touch with, the domain of affectivity, the domain of feeling.[15] His guideposts are those of theory in aesthetics, and he integrates aesthetic theory with the work of McClellan on the motivational status of achievement and of Berlyne on conflict and curiosity as motivational concepts. From this integration he derives explanations of motivation, learning, and teaching. A key concept in this integration is that of discrepancy, to which he devotes an entire chapter.[16] To summarize his definition of discrepancy in my words, we

89

may say that it is the feeling-tone established when one encounters that which is novel, perceives the juxtaposition of incongruous elements, experiences surprise when the expected does not occur. Although Arnstine does not mention it, his concept of discrepancy is very similar to, though treating of feeling rather than cognition, current dissonance theory in psychology and Creegan's "psychology of shock." [17] But note again the definition of discrepancy: discrepancy is a feeling-tone, and this feeling-tone is at the center of his discussion of motivation, teaching, learning, and certain related assumptions regarding the nature of knowledge.

Although I applaud Arnstine for his bringing feeling back into the center of considerations of teaching and knowing without slipping into the morass of mysticism, his formulations have been almost entirely derived from aesthetics and psychology, and his implied goal does not differentiate his efforts from the sociological-nomothetic tradition. His implied goal is to develop general statements which would permit the handling of the domain of affectivity in much the same manner in which statements regarding other rational categories are treated. Arnstine focused his inquiry on the right place but, then, did not change the basic nature of the inquiry itself. Operating within the limits of steno-language, though he appears to be attempting to break away from that with his examples from art, one could not expect a very radical breakthrough in his proposals for a philosophy of education. In respect to his deriving his formulations from aesthetics and certain movements in contemporary psychology, he just may be on the right track. Before conceding, however, that a workable conception of knowledge and knowing for education, which incorporates as an integral part of its structure the category *feeling,* can only come from aesthetics and psychology, we should take at least one more look to epistemology—specifically, an investigation of the possibilities for education of an epistemological paradigm derived from the philosophy of Albert Camus.

Camus' obsession was with the development of a moral philosophy, though he denied that he was attempting this in a systematic way. Some, such as Chiaromonte,[18] have contended that no one of the present generation has analyzed with greater clarity the intellectual and moral implications of our modern situation. Following Camus' involvement with the question of morality, most students of his thought have concerned themselves with explications and extensions of his thought. But, Camus also addressed himself to the question of knowledge. In *The Myth of Sisyphus*,[19] in the section in which he sets forth his method of analysis, he also treats of the problem of knowledge, not only what can be known, but also how we may come to know. *The Rebel*, which has been considered almost exclusively as a work in moral philosophy, may be considered, just as well, as an extensive analysis of the consequences of those philosophic positions which have held that knowledge of the absolute is possible. It is true that Camus does not give primary attention to the question of knowledge; neither have students of his thought. But, in setting forth his method of analysis, he works through a paradigm case which demonstrates the necessary relationship between feeling and knowledge. It is this paradigm case which holds considerable promise for philosophy of education. An understanding of the case, however, is contingent upon an understanding of certain preliminary, and more general, considerations regarding his epistemology.

As indicated in the comment regarding *The Rebel*, Camus rejects any notion of absolute knowledge; in that work the rejection is based on the consequences of such epistemological claims. Earlier, however, in *The Myth of Sisyphus*, his rejection of claims of absolute knowledge was based on an analysis of the logic of absolutistic statements about truth and about the unity of reality. He finds the arguments to be incomplete and self-contradictory. Camus will not, on the other hand, accept the extreme of irrationalism, that extreme which has had so much appeal for certain of the existentialists. He analyzes the arguments of several leading existentialists who have adopted irrationalism, demonstrating that they in their arguments, contradict their own arguments. Camus is asserting, therefore, that the world is neither rational nor irrational. By this he means that to assert that the world is either rational or irrational is to assert that the world will accommodate itself to man's categories of thought; this is to further assert that man is capable of accounting for the total range of phenomena of the world. What alternative does Camus leave us?

He says that the world is reasonable as opposed to rational. By this he means that reason may be used as a tool for helping us make some sense of the world of our experience, but claiming neither totality nor truth, and always operating within very tightly drawn limits, limits which may be labelled sensation, perception, and construction. The first assertion in Camus' epistemology is that all knowledge comes from sensory experience. All else follows from this. The knowledge obtained from sensory experience is tentative, relative, and amenable to human consciousness; that is, such knowledge is subject to manipulation by the tools of human reason. Though the original sensory experience may be manipulated by human reason, the end result of that manipulation is merely a construction and has no special ontological status. It should be noted at this point that Camus uses the terms *sensory experience* and *sensation* to refer to all raw-feels, to all immediately perceived feelings, without regard to the origin of the stimuli, whether "inside" the organism or "outside" the organism. Camus' primary referent for all his assertions is the experiencing-body, and he is very careful not to fragment man's knowledge from his body as traditional and modern Western philosophies have done. This note of caution at this point is needed, for his use of the terms mentioned has caused some to associate his thinking with certain British positivists. Even Sartre [20] has made this error. It is an easy one to make, for, when Camus asserts that knowledge is limited to sensory experience, he is not far from Ayer's contention that knowledge is constructed from that which is perceivable or capable of being perceived. Since it is the case that knowledge is limited to bodily-sensory experience, no special validity for abstract labels and/or categories is allowed. Human consciousness, for Camus, simply records, simply describes. In *The Stranger*, for example, nothing is explained; no synthesis occurs; the consciousness is fed only short, descriptive bits, and the only certainty consists of those short, descriptive bits of any particular moment of experience.

We may attempt, of course, explanation of these "bits." In philosophic terms which are more traditional, we may construct categories, laws, and ordered realms of being, but none of these constitutes knowledge; they are, rather, *constructions* from that which is given in sensory experience.

In a somewhat poetic manner Camus summarizes these points when he says,

> This heart within me I can feel, and I judge that it exists. This world I can touch, and I likewise judge that it exists. There ends all my knowledge, and the rest is construction.[21]

Camus, however, has no objection to the act of mental construction in itself, and, thus, he has no objection to the work of most Western philosophers, though the consequences of that work sometimes terrify him. It must not be forgotten that he himself was a student of the Greeks, having written his thesis on Plotinus. What he does object to is a mistake in Western philosophy which has had murderous results, namely, making the judgment that the constructions—categories, laws, First Principles, etc.—are more real than the constructors. Hence, Camus would not argue with one's concern with systems of logic, of explanation, of language analysis, of metaphysics, of theology even —so long as one does not forget these are mere constructions, intellectual games, which, when taken seriously, in Sartre's sense of seriousness, eventuate in murder.

What then can we know? Further, what bearings might this conception of knowledge have on education defined as first-person experience? Let us approach these two questions by returning to the paradigm case referred to earlier. In *The Myth of Sisyphus*,[22] Camus distinguishes between the feeling of absurdity and the notion of absurdity. He also indicates the relationships between the two. His concern, of course, was with the concept of absurdity, and students of his thought have followed that lead. But, what he has also set forth is an epistemological formula, and, as such, the primary terms are no longer the two terms of absurdity, but are the terms *feeling* and *notion*. Our question then becomes, what is the nature of, and the relationship between, the feeling of any X and the notion of the same X?

The feeling of an X may include a wide variety of sensations, ranging from what was referred to earlier as rawfeels to high specific emotions, but no special requirement is placed on the specificity of focus or on the identifiability of the stimulus. Notions of that X arise out of our attempts to deal with the feeling at some level of thought. This priority of feeling has been recognized by a few over the years, but among philosophers, as pointed out earlier, it has been generally held that feeling was not a component of knowledge itself, and among psychologists, the common view has been that feeling was only incidentally related to the process of learning and not relevant at all to either empirical or rational "laws" of learning. In recent years, certain persons have begun to recognize that human feeling must be included in explanations of human experience. The psychologist Schutz,[23] representing a minority point of view of course, has asserted that bodily-feel is actually a type of pre-logical thinking necessary to the act of making decisions. The thesis of the latest work of the philosopher Langer [24] is that feeling is *the* basis for a theory of mind. And the communications theorist McLuhan [25] finds some amusement in the fact that when the scholars and physicists of our time penetrate to the lowest levels of non-literate (non-written language) awareness, they are confronted with some of the most advanced and sophisticated ideas of twentieth-century art and science. The pre-predicative, non-naming, non-mediated sectors of ordinary experience are the starting points and integral features of human knowledge. Although the point is beginning to be seen by persons from different disciplines, it has been Camus who has made the emphasis explicit and who has provided a paradigm for talking about feeling and knowledge.

Notions of X, hence, are nothing more than our attempts to describe and explain our feelings of X. These notions may range from prayers and poetry to common sense and mathematico-deductive explanations. They may range from our attempts to cope with highly generalized feelings of anxiety about man's place in the universe to a specific emotion of curiosity about the movements of certain subatomic particles. But note that the progression is always from the feeling to the notion. Note further that the notion is always a construction about the feeling and never exhausts fully the "meaning" of the feeling itself; this is not a technical point at all. Anyone who has ever tried to tell another about some personal experience—a sunrise over the Maine coast, the vibrations of sex, or a personal tragedy, for example—knows of the difficulty, of the impossibility, of translating the feelings, the sensory experience, into declarative sentences.

The pattern of the development of Camus' thought on a specific point will illustrate well the progression from feeling to notion. In the development of his notion of absurdity, he first noticed a certain awareness of dissonance within himself; this he discussed with others and found that they too had experienced similar feelings. He then proceeded from the level of everyday life to one level of abstraction from that; he wrote a play, *Caligula,* in which he had his characters grapple with these feelings of discrepancy. He then wrote a novel, *The Stranger,* which was one more level of abstraction from the level of actual experience. Last of all, he wrote *The Myth of Sisyphus* in which he sets forth both his method of analysis and the results of that analysis of the feeling of absurdity. Each step in the development of the notion was a very cautious move away from the level of actual human feeling.

And yet, there is some sort of necessity, which everyone with the exception of the extreme mystic recognizes, for moving from feeling to notion. Camus' criticism is that Western man has pursued that necessity to the point of cutting the notion of X off from the original feeling of X. We have then treated these notions, which it must remembered are but constructions and have no special reality status, as the substance of knowledge and force them on the students of the world. When the student can make the appropriate notional responses to the notional stimuli, we say the student has grasped the "knowledge" of a particular discipline. (And then we wonder why the retention curve drops as it does so very quickly.) Given the framework of the feeling/notion paradigm, knowledge is the coherent-feeling-of-X-notion-of-X-gestalt. Given the paradigm, coming to know any X is to work an integration of my feelings of that X and the possible notions of that X, progressing from feeling to notion, and moving toward higher levels of refinement of integration, that is, toward greater degrees of coherence.

What does all this have to say in respect to epistemology and in respect to educational methodology? In respect to epistemology, all knowledge begins in a particular experiencing-body. But there is a world "out there," for I can touch it; I can construct notions about it, notions ranging from simple descriptions to elaborate explanations. It is not a world which I project with something called my mind. But my knowledge of the world arises out of my feelings of being out of harmony with the world, of dissatisfaction with my lack of notions about the world, of passionate, persistent anger with the world because it won't reveal as much about itself as I desire. This knowledge of the world is not simply a matter of my checking my feelings against the world with some sort of correspondence test. My feelings are at every point bound up, with, and in notions of that world. Given a conception of the world as having inherent meaning and lawfulness, then a correspondence test becomes relevant. But, given a contemporary physical scientist's conception of the world, that is, one which is ultimately discussed in metaphor, and given that I am both in and of this world, a correspondence test becomes inadequate, becomes futile. And to talk of a dichotomy between the knower and the known is to play but another game of notions with its idealist trap, emphasis on the knower, and its realist pitfall, emphasis on the known. Knowledge is my feeling/notion gestalt.

But is there any sense in which one can say that a given feeling/notion gestalt is true or false? The question is important not only to epistemology *qua* epistemology, but the answer will also bear heavily on our conceptions of authority, of the role of the expert, and of the function of the teacher. Consider the case of the man who holds that the earth is flat. He has certain body-feels as to up and down, east and west, over and under, earth and sky, etc. At an articulable level, these feelings may be expressed as a belief that the earth is flat. His notions are consistent with, in coherence with, his feelings and may be reinforced by his religion and local folklore. But he is obviously in error, you say; he needs information, guidance, and attitude modification, the typical school personnel may say. But does he speak falsely? And does his flat-earth notion constitute the grounds for claiming an educational need? The man may hold to his flat-earth notion for a lifetime, functioning during that lifetime as a father, a lover, a husband, a business man, a deputy sheriff, and a football coach, among other things, and functioning in each case with success. Now, if the man should choose to be an astronaut, the picture would change considerably. He would need different notions regarding the shape of the earth, not because authority told him of his "ignorance," but because the pre-determining feelings had changed. He now possesses the feelings of an astronaut, feelings of curiosity about space, about space physics, and about living in space. With these feelings it would be mandatory that he have a different set of notions. Which set of notions, then, is true? The question is meaningless, for notions, cut off from their feeling-origins, are nothing more than intellectual games, games which may be amusing to play but which do not inform in any new way about ordinary experience. The terms of truth and falsity, hence, are two more from our Western intellectual tradition to be discarded by the wayside of history. Feeling/notion gestalts have functional value in given episodes of experience, and, when the experience changes so that the gestalt no longer possesses such value, new gestalts will be formed.

Further, it is the experiencing-body in any given episode of experience which says that the gestalt has such value or not; this is not a solipsism; this is not subjectivism. If a person had a round-football-field notion, to use a ludicrous example, it isn't likely that he would ever become a successful football coach. But, if he lived in Tibet, he could believe what he wanted to about the shape of football fields, and it would not make any difference. Should he decide to introduce football into Tibet, however, his notions would have to change. What must be kept in mind is a point that was emphasized in the first chapter, namely, that to talk meaningfully about human experience one must attempt to do that from the perspective of the individual, not from the perspective of any rational category. What may be quite meaningful in ordinary experience may be non-meaningful in terms of rational thought. In short, we may claim to have a knowledge of the world which is objective, which transcends ordinary experience, but that knowledge which makes a difference in the ordinary experience of the individual is knowledge which is distinctly human, meaning by this, limited to ordinary experience. In education, therefore, that knowledge of most worth is human knowledge.

There is obviously a certain take-it-or-leave-it attitude about such knowledge claims, and several writers have touched on the point but without treating it explicitly. Wheelwright,[26] for example, says that the "truth" of a diaphoric metaphor is given in the moment of experience in a take-it-or-leave-it manner; there is neither formal nor empirical proof appropriate to the case of a diaphoric metaphor. Sartre, in his discussion of Camus' character Meursault,[27] says that Camus makes no attempt to explain or to justify that which is inherently unjustifiable, that is, Meursault's experience. That experience *is,* and one can either take it or leave it, but one's taking it or leaving it will not affect the reality of that experience at all. And, as a different kind of example, Olafson [28] criticizes the existentialists for their use of metaphors which are not amenable to the conceptual analyses popular with British and American philosophers, for, to Olafson's chagrin, such metaphors of experience simply defy the rules of conceptual analysis; they possess that take-it-or-leave-it "attitude" which stands without rational justification. And knowledge, defined as my feeling/notion gestalt, is of this order.

Knowledge and Educational Method

Certain of the implications for educational practice derived from various epistemologies and learning theories have already been mentioned. The attention, at this point, is to the suggestions for educational method which might be obtained from the radically restructured conception of knowledge set forth above. In respect to education, three suggestions have already been made. The first of these is that there are distinct limits to knowledge claims; no special validity can be claimed for large conceptual schemes, such as a particular design of history or some quantitative formulation from theoretical physics. These are highly sophisticated notions and probably should be taught, but they should be taught for what they are: highly sophisticated notions and nothing more.

A second suggestion concerns the matter of motivation. Perhaps, in respect to motivation, we are to a new view of Dewey's concern with student-interest, but interest in the framework of the feeling/notion paradigm is something more than merely a starting point for instruction, as something more than a psychological prerequisite for learning.

Interest is the action taken to overcome the dissonance created by discrepancies between our feelings and our notions. Motivation, conceived of in these terms, becomes more than the starting device of instruction; it becomes the very process of learning and becomes its own method. But the method of dissonance prescribes no particular techniques. If dissonance can be aroused with lectures, lecture; with group discussions, have them. If dissonance leads to the project method as a way of achieving the coherent feeling/notion gestalt, use that method. If dissonance leads to programmed instruction, program and reinforce; to field trips, make them; to film-making, photograph. And, if it leads to an individual's quiet probing into the depths of his own self and eventuating in poetry, painting, or dance, encourage him.

The third suggestion, which is really an extension of the second, concerns additional aspects of the process of coming to know. As indicated earlier in the chapter, learning theorists have written much about the nature of learning, of coming to know; almost always, however, a Lockean epistemology has been assumed even though the learning theorists differed widely among themselves. This common assumption holds that knowledge is independent of the knower, that the mind is empty or blank, and that coming to know consists of certain operations of "bombardment" of the organism. Kilpatrick,[29] attempting to correct this simplistic, linear conception of learning, coined the term *simultaneous learnings* to refer to the fact that, while learning certain factual matters, the student is also learning certain attitudes and is making judgments regarding the appropriateness of those factual matters for his life. Kilpatrick's attempted correction is in the right direction, but he did not go far enough. Body-feels are not merely simultaneous learnings; rather, they are the origin, the means, and the end of all that is learned. Coming to know is to work an integration of feelings of that X with the possible notions of the same X, and the order, feeling to notion, is always the same. By movement toward greater degrees of integration, I mean the achieving of greater degrees of coherence between feeling and notion. In case of certain specific feelings, such as curiosity about a particular matter, the feeling of that X may come into complete coherence

99

quickly and easily. On more complex sets of feelings, such as those having to do with social relations and man's place in the universe, the feeling/notion coherence will not be easily achieved, if it is achieved at all.

Does all of this mean that subject matter, of which libraries and professors' heads are filled, is to be discarded as well? No, but it does mean that the status and uses of subject matter will be altered considerably. Subject matter will no longer be considered an end in itself for students to "master" in some sense. Instead, subject matter, of which the teacher will need to have much at his fingertips, will serve two primary functions: 1) to create dissonance, and 2) to provide alternative notions. There will be little, if any, concern with covering a given amount of material, though the course may be organized about a given set of topics which the students are to encounter in a course, and there will be little attention given to the essential structures of a discipline unless a student desires such in his struggle for his own feeling/notion gestalts. The teacher, then, will be one who is quite well versed in his subject matter, aware all the while that his notions are the results of certain of his own feelings; he studied mathematics, for example, because of certain curiosities, excitements, etc., of his own. In short, this means that the teacher will not be conceived of as a teacher of mathematics, but will be a mathematician, who shares with his students all the curiosity, the excitement, the occasional boredom, the challenges, the life-style of an experiencing-body whose intended meanings are couched, not just in the steno-language of mathematics, but in the entire range of existential language.

Chapter VI

EXPLANATION AND COUNSELING

The Language of Explaining and Counseling

A student—or client, or counselee, or patient, depending on one's terminological bias—walks into the counselor's office and indicates that he has a social, learning, vocational, or personal problem. Several counseling sessions may be required for the so-called problem to be identified, and the mentioned indication of the problem may be provided by a variety of signals, both direct and inferred. The client brings with him all the multi-dimensional, simultaneous, protean characteristics of the moment plus a unique and complex history plus goals for the future which may be quite vague or quite sharply defined. In addition to similar sets of characteristics, the counselor brings to the sessions certain conceptual and other tools for clarifying and explaining and predicting the client's behavior, with each of these three functions receiving different emphasis depending on the theoretical orientation of the counselor. Now we have arrived at a critical turn, for what does each of these terms mean? And what theoretical orientation is most valid in answering the question of meaning and that of emphasis? By the term *clarifying* do we mean creating awareness on the part of the client through intra-personal or inter-personal communication? Or do we refer to a process of testing, evaluating, and consulting past records to clarify the client's present situation? Or, something entirely different? By the term *explaining* do we refer to a search for antecedent conditions, for explanatory laws of behavior, or to something else again? By the term *predicting* do we refer to a process of interpreting a contingency table of some type, or to an analysis of motives, or to something else? To bring some degree of order into this array of questions, the counselor will utilize a model of explanation of human behavior, either explicitly stated or implied in a more general counseling theory.

There is no want for such theories, for models of counseling operation: learning theory models of conditioning and extinction, psychoanalytic models, vocational-fit models —to suggest the dominant ones. But counseling psychologists continue to grope for a model of operation which will take into account, which will provide the language and conceptual tools for, the uniquely human, experiential aspects of their work. Both counseling and clinical psychologists have had difficulty in appropriating laboratory and computer models to the distinctly human, idiographic characteristics of their clients. Counseling psychologists, in particular, have found the greater difficulty, for they are supposedly working with "normal" subjects; that is, subjects without severe perceptual impairment, cognitive disorganization, or affective repression. And it is this range of "normal" subjects which makes up the major portion of the workload of the typical school counselor.

What do the three dominant theories, or models, say to the school counselor? In common, they all assume general laws of explanation of human behavior, though they differ as to the specific nature and content of the laws. Since they are all concerned with covering statements of explanation, they are all nomothetic. For example, the counselor with a learning theory orientation will most likely emphasize the role of objective tests, of comparisons with normative data, of case histories to determine the behaviors of the counselee in earlier, yet similar, situations, and actuarial diagnosis and prediction. He will, in short, stress being "scientific." The counselee's problem will be solved by rewarding more appropriate behavior or by redirection of overt behaviors. The counselee, or client, is one who yields highly specific responses to stimuli, cues, signs, etc., and whose changes in behavior, i.e., learnings, are affected by the degree of drive reduction (Hull), by trial and error (Thorndike), by redirection of movements (Guthrie), or by the application of an appropriate reinforcement schedule (Skinner). But whether one speaks of drive reduction, or of trial and error learning, or of redirection of movements, or of reinforcement schedules, he is speaking of approaches to the explanation of human behavior which assume, first, that general, explanatory laws are possible and, second, that such explanatory statements are now available. The same two assumptions are shared by psychoanalytic and vocational-fit models. The counselor with a psychoanalytic orientation assumes even before the client walks in the door that the client's personality is made up of certain id, ego, and superego functions, operating according to the life and death instincts, and functioning inadequately— hence, a problem—because of certain improper handlings at specifiable developmental stages. The counselor "knows" all this before he has ever seen the particular client, because, according to his assumptions, each person is a particularization of the general, explanatory laws postulated in psychoanalytic theory. Vocational-fit models, which have been dominant primarily in vocational guidance, lead to a type of counseling in which highly specific analyses are made of various job operations, objective analysis of the client is conducted with the use of special tests, and then the counselor's task is to determine whether or not the two sets of data "fit." Although vocational-fit models are much less sophisticated, at the level of theory, than the other two, the nomothetic assumption regarding explanation is the same. The counselor approaches the client from the position of general statements which are assumed to be adequate for clarifying, explaining, and predicting, the particular client's case.

Since the three dominant models for counseling—learning theory, psychoanalytic, and vocational-fit—are nomothetic, the language of each is of the type identified earlier as standardized or steno-language. The basic terms, whether words and sentences or numbers and formulas, have prescribed meanings which are imposed upon the meaning of the life, of the ordinary experience, of the particular client. Research conducted from the perspective of either of these orientations is always couched in the terms of steno-language. A perusal of the American Psychological Association's *Journal of Counseling Psychology* will illustrate the point well. The American Personnel and Guidance Association's *Personnel and Guidance Journal* will also illustrate the point. As a result of research couched in the terms of steno-language, the simultaneous aspects of ordinary experience are ignored, and nothing appears in the journals about them with the exception of an occasional admission that certain impressionistic data were also obtained. But, as we shall see later, when impressionistic data have been obtained, the assumption is that either now or later such data can be brought under the general covering statements. It would appear on the surface that the work of Carl Rogers, Abraham Maslow, and others of the so-called "third force" in psychology would differ significantly from the three orientations discussed to this point. In many respects this is true, but, as will be seen, that third force does not possess a coherent theory—it is more an amalgam of shared values—and, hence, has not made explicit its own implied nomothetic assumption. Prior to the discussion of the third force in psychology, however, this chapter will concern itself with the more commonly held views regarding the explanation of human behavior. Following these two considerations, the chapter will then move to an examination of the possibilities of explanation of ordinary experience, using the conceptual tools of existential language.

Explanation in Counseling

One of the most highly sophisticated attempts in psychology to explain human behavior was that of Hull and associates at Yale in the 1930's. The attempt resulted in the book, *Mathematico-Deductive Theory of Rote Learning,*[1] which was subtitled, "A Study in Scientific Methodology."[2] The book first provides an essay on theoretical methodology, then sets forth a brief description of the methods of obtaining empirical data from rote-learning experiments, approximately forty pages of postulates are then given, after which follows over two hundred pages of theorems. An imposing exercise in mathematical deduction it certainly is. But what are Hull and his associates saying about explanation? They are saying that human behaviors are instances of natural laws and can be both explained in terms of and predicted from those laws.[3] In fact, they leave no doubt that postulates are natural laws. Given knowledge of such laws, then behaviors, which are but instantilizations of those laws, can be predicted. Meehl refers to this position as methodological determinism,[4] as opposed to metaphysical determinism, and says that psychologists share this position with all practitioners of the natural sciences. Methodological determinism holds, says Meehl, that "If these laws hold strictly, well and good; if they are at best probabilistic, we will settle for that, since they will still be very useful." [5] It further holds that, since human behavior demonstrates the regularity of laws, then that behavior is "susceptible of rational causal explanations." [6]

A more recent statement of the same position is that by Kerlinger [7] who, in a section on explanation and theory, states that the goal of research is theory and that the purpose of theory is to specify the lawful relationships among phenomena, thus enabling prediction of the phenomena. For him, theoretical explanation necessarily implies prediction, and he speaks in negative tones of those whose research does not push toward the attainment of those most general, covering statements of human behavior.

If the goal of research is theory and if the purpose of theory is to explain and predict, all of which Meehl has called methodological determinism, just how does this explanation take place? What does it mean to explain? The work of Nagel is helpful at this point. [8] From the point of view of common sense, explanations are offered to satisfy "Why?" questions. If I leave a theatre to discover that the sidewalks and streets are wet, I may answer the question, "Why are the streets wet?" by "explaining" that rain has been falling. Or perhaps I am on my way to lecture to a class when I see one of my students walking away from the building in which the class is held. I hail him and ask why he is walking away from the classroom. He may "explain" that he thought I was out of town, or that he is ill, or that he could spend his time more profitably golfing. Whatever his reason, I now have an "explanation" for his behavior. Nagel [9] recognizes this common sense type of explanation but suggests that scientific explanations offer responses to questions relating explanatory assumptions to their explicanda (the things which are explained) in distinct, logical patterns. He sets forth four such patterns, two of which, the deductive and probabilistic, have been dominant in psychological theories.

Nagel's deductive pattern is fashioned much on the order of formal, deductive logic, involving the usual deduction of conclusions from major and minor premises. Deductive *explanations,* however, must meet, according to Nagel, two conditions other than the logical one: these two are the substantive and epistemic conditions. The substantive conditions provide content for the major premise, minor premise, and the conclusion. Thus, in a deductive explanation, the form will be that of deductive logic while the content will include general law(s), instantial statement(s), and the explicandum. The explanation, then, must contain all the general laws and all the instantial statements which are necessary to deduce the explicandum. To illustrate with one of Nagel's examples, we may ask, "Why did moisture form on the outside of the glass when it was filled with ice yesterday?" The explanation would contain one general law, namely, that whenever the temperature of any volume of air containing water vapor is reduced below the point where the density of vapor in the air is greater than the saturation density of water vapor in air at that temperature, the vapor in the air condenses into liquid water at those places where the temperature of the air has dropped below the saturation point. Other laws are assumed, of course, laws pertaining to water, glass, and the temperature saturation density relationship. Three instantial statements are also needed to explain the moisture's forming on the glass yesterday: the volume of air surrounding the glass yesterday contained water vapor; the temperature of the layer of air immediately adjacent to the glass was reduced when ice water was poured into the glass; and, the actual density of vapor in this layer of air when its temperature dropped was greater than the saturation density at the new temperature. Given the general law and the instantial statements, it will necessarily follow that moisture did, and in the future will, form on the glass. Nagel has both explained the matter and provided the basis for prediction.

The epistemic conditions demand that the universal laws and instantial statements must be "true" in that they be supported by sufficient empirical evidence. Nagel makes the point that the terms *sufficient* and *adequate* merely require that there be no empirical evidence for regarding the premise as false while there must be some empirical evidence to support it. But it is not enough that the premises follow logical form and are true. The major premise must be causal, or a law of nature, rather than merely expressing "accidental" or *de facto* universality. An example should make the point clear.

All the nails in Smith's house are rusty.
N is a nail in Smith's house.
Therefore, N is rusty.

In this example, the major premise, All the nails in Smith's house are rusty, asserts no more than accidental universality. As Nagel points out, the connection between antecedent and consequent conditions must involve necessity in order for a law to obtain, although this necessity is variously conceived and is described by such qualifying adjectives as logical, causal, physical, and real. Nagel suggests that a test for such universality is the substitution of the subjunctive conditional for the present indicative: "For any X, if X were copper and were heated, then X would expand . . . On the other hand, the patently accidental universal 'All nails in Smith's house are rusty' does not justify the subjunctive conditional." [10] It is quite possible that a nail could be replaced by a new, shiny one. We cannot say that "All nails in Smith's house *would* be rusty" in view of possible replacement.

Explanations of the probabilistic type differ from the deductive pattern in at least two respects. The statistical law, which provides the content for the major premise in the probabilistic model, is an assertion based on known properties of a given population. Secondly, although the probabilistic model follows the pattern of formal deduction, no necessary, causal connection is implied; thus, the explicandum will never be stated in terms of necessity, only in terms of probability. Nagel illustrates from history an explanation of the probabilistic type. The major premise is: In ancient Rome the probability was high that an individual belonging to the upper strata of society and possessed by great hatred of tyranny would plot the death of men who were in position to secure tyrannical power. Nagel uses two instantial statements: Cassius was such a Roman, and Caesar was such a potential tyrant. Nagel's conclusion (explicandum): though it does not follow that Cassius plotted the death of Caesar, it is highly probable that he did so. Some psychologists, such as Hull, have attempted the exclusive use of the deductive pattern of explanation, but most American psychologists have found the probabilistic pattern, because of its use of statistical laws for major premises, more to their liking. But more on that later.

Let us look further at the matter of explanation of historical phenomena, for, when such explanation has been delimited to the history of the individual, it has been used with great frequency by psychologists. Although Nagel has used historical materials as examples, one of which was given above, Carl Hempel deals more directly with the matter, especially the role and status of general laws in historical explanation. Hempel describes a general law as "a statement of universal conditional form which is capable of being confirmed or disconfirmed by suitable empirical findings." [11] He states further that general laws in natural science function primarily to connect events in patterns of explanation and prediction. To this point, his description appears to be limited to Nagel's deductive model. Hempel, however, does not insist on the rigid epistemic requirements demanded by Nagel for deductive explanation. For this reason, Hempel's explanation, though logically deductive, may be superimposed on either the deductive or probabilistic model, depending on the nature of the general laws. If they are true, we use the deductive model. If they are probable (statistically "true"), the probabilistic model may be employed. Historical explanation of this type would show, says Hempel, that the events in question were not merely matters of chance, but were to be expected in view of certain antecedent conditions. "The expectation referred to is not prophecy or divination, but rational scientific anticipation which rests on the assumption of general laws." [12] Foreseeing certain difficulties in the formulation of general laws in historical analysis (namely, assumed familiarity with common psychology and with statistical frequencies of the time), Hempel suggests that an explanatory sketch might be developed which could be filled out as more empirical evidence is discovered.

When the process of explanation set forth by Hempel is delimited to the history of individuals, we find an approach to explanation used by psychologists of psychoanalytic and behavioristic orientations, which means most American psychologists. This approach to explanation has usually been subsumed under the rubric *historical determinism,* an assumption that past events provide the basis for explanation of current actions and attitudes. Given this assumption as the basis of explanation, a counselor, for example, will attempt to determine the history of a particular client in order to find a reasonable explanation of the client's present problem; the educational psychologist will search the history of the learner in an attempt to find the "why" of present learning difficulties; and, the teacher will look to the past for evidences of social conflict which, according to the assumption, has its origins in the past and has a causal connection with the misbehavior of the present. The argument is that, if we possess an adequate knowledge of antecedent conditions, we can confidently diagnose the present difficulty and predict subsequent behavior. The antecedent conditions may consist of environmental factors, conditioning schedules, or the resolution of certain developmental stages as in psychoanalysis. Hence, in very concrete ways the work of psychological theorists such as Hull and Meehl, of behavioral research specialists such as Kerlinger, and of philosophers such as Nagel and Hempel comes to bear on the practice of education.

Explanation Humanized?

Alternative schemes of explanation have been offered by those who oppose the type of explanation described to this point, that is, explaining human behavior in terms of larger covering statements. The criticism has generally held that such explanation may be appropriate for non-human objects but not for human subjects. More specifically, the criticism has taken two forms: that the explicandum should be human action rather than human behavior; that that which is being explained should be the perceptual world of the client rather than merely behavior. The criticism, then, basically is an attack on the reductionistic orientation in psychology which has focused on behavior and defined behavior as highly specific muscle movements. Let us see what the critics would have us do by way of explanation.

One of the most thorough, recent analyses of the matter is that of A. Louch in his book *Explanation and Human Action.*[13] The work is a frontal attack on the notion that explanation is subsumption under some covering statement, such as a general law or hypothesis. Louch argues that everyday explanations of human actions are often particular, not general, and that all psychology can do is to extend in limited ways what this everyday explanation already does, that is, explain/appraise human behavior in its changing contexts.[14] Neither psychology nor philosophy can provide us with a set of general rules about how and why human behavior arises. Earlier (Chapters I and III), Louch argues that the Humean-derived approach to explanation will not even hold for non-animate nature. We do observe particular causal links, as, for example, the collision of two cars, but there is no reason why we must see particulars of this type as being subsumptions under general laws. The Humean-derived model has hypnotized us, as Louch puts it, so that we tend to see particulars as antecedent and consequent terms of a general law. He then works through several common examples to substantiate his point. But what does he offer as an alternative? He says that the focus must be shifted from behavior to action, a more molar term which includes not only the muscle-behavior but the underlying motive as well. If we understand the motive, then we can appraise/explain the action. Or, as he puts it in one discussion, "Assigning a motive is showing that circumstances warrant actions." [15] Terms such as appraise and warrant begin to fill the lexicon of Louch's notion of explanation to the extent that he calls his a moral explanation. But without getting involved in that thicket, the key feature is that explanation is to be done in terms of motives, desires, etc. All of this would seem to indicate a much more "human" explanation than that derived from Hume and contemporary philosophers of science, but his reconstruction is not radically human at all; he continues to grant the validity of explanatory models which will do for the human sciences what the Humean model has done for the physical. To shift from behaviors to motives as the raw data for empirical premises is to both grant the validity of the basic approach and extremely complicate the obtaining of the raw data, that is, the motives, desires, intentions, etc. Further, to shift from describing and explaining to appraising and warranting is to make of explanation a moral enterprise; in so doing, Louch may have opened new avenues of inquiry, but, also in so doing, he has transferred the matter of human behavior into an area that is even less equipped conceptually, after hundreds of years of inquiry, than the one he is leaving.

Louch has not been alone, however, in his attempt to explain in terms of motives. One book,[16] which claims to present a comprehensive theory for explaining human behavior, is of special relevance, for it was written as a theory of explanation for counselors, as opposed to one written for philosophers of psychological theorists. These authors also argue that molecular conceptions of behavior are inadequate for explaining the action of "normal" humans, and they also, with Louch, assert that the focus should be on motives rather than on overt behavior. Their thinking, however, is not as alert as Louch's to the difficulties, both logical and empirical, entailed in attempts to explain human behavior; thus, they assume a strictly, deductive form, changing merely the content-terms in the form but without indicating just how the connections are to be made among the new terms. The first chapter of the book sets forth the postulates, which Barry and Wolf call "Universal Motivating Forces;" in a very loose manner, they derive a lower order which they call "Subsidiary Motives;" [17] then, after setting up this network of *a priori* assumptions, they attempt to locate the individual in that network. Although I commend their goal of achieving a genuinely "human" theory of explanation, they have claimed too much, epistemologically, for their universal statements and have concerned themselves little at all with the logical connections within their deductive form. More on this later.

But what of the so-called third force in American psychology? Does it not provide a more genuinely human approach to the explanation of behavior? Is not one of its primary attacks on attempts to adapt physical models of explanation to human behavior/action? On the surface, it would appear that the third force does reject physical models and does look for a pattern of explanation which accounts for those variables which are distinctly human, but a closer examination, however, will demonstrate that, though the third force does not possess a single set of assumptions, the works of its major spokesman are clearly nomothetic and deductive in form.

111

Before getting into the examination, an additional word of identification of this third force may be helpful. The so-called third force is made up of many diverse streams of thought which have tended to polarize into a loose identity in its opposition to the dominant streams of thought in American psychology, namely, behaviorism and psychoanalysis. One can trace the various streams of thought by beginning with the German gestaltists and phenomenologists and moving to contemporary existential therapists. This is the humanistic wing of American psychology, or, as is sometimes put derisively, the soft underbelly of psychology. One of its distinctive features has been that most of the psychologists associated with this movement have been primarily clinicians or counselors, those who have had to grapple on a daily basis with actual human problems. Some of its more influential writings include Rogers' *Counseling and Psychotherapy* (1942) and *Client-Centered Therapy* (1951), Snygg and Combs' *Individual Behavior* (1949) which was discussed briefly in Chapter One, May's *The Meaning of Anxiety* (1950) and *Existential Psychology* (1961), Maslow's *Motivation and Personality* (1954), and Lyons' *Psychology and the Measure of Man* (1963). Although the third force has no official journal, *The Journal of Humanistic Psychology* and *Existential Psychiatry* are two which receive greatest attention. Thus, although the third force represents a minority position in American psychology, it is one of the dominant, if not the dominant, influence in counseling circles, especially school counseling.

While the charge that schemes of explanation in the third force are just as nomothetic and deductive as the models of Hull and Nagel can be brought against the work of Maslow and that of Snygg and Combs, among others, the focus of the criticism will be on Rogers, for it has been his work which has come to bear most influentially on the practice of school counseling. His terms *client-centered therapy* and *non-directive counseling* have become favorite cliches among counselors and counselor educators, cliches possessing, for the faithful, the magical power of self-definition. Glanz, for example, without any supporting argument or evidence, simply asserts the known truth to the faithful when he says, "The nature of all counseling demands that it be client-centered." [18] But to return to Rogers, at about the same time that Hull and his associates were developing and setting forth their mathematico-deductive model of explanation, Rogers was setting forth what appeared to be an entirely different conception of explanation. In *Counseling and Psychotherapy*, he took what was interpreted to be a very audacious step, setting forth an approach to explanation which was in the philosophic-phenomenological tradition rather than in the experimental-scientific one. But it must be noted, that though the intellectual traditions were quite at variance, he was nonetheless setting forth a method of explanation; explanation was still his goal, and he made the point very clear in a later work.[19]

The statement of his nineteen propositions,[20] with their emphasis on individual experience and on internal frames of reference, would appear to be an attempt at establishing the basis for an understanding of the ordinary experience of individuals, and many have used his propositions in this manner. But, from the beginning, Rogers had precise explanation in mind and, in more recent works, has re-emphasized that goal. At a symposium held in 1959, Rogers,[21] reflecting on the apparent split in psychology between what he called the objective trend, on one hand, and the existential trend, on the other, saw no great difficulty in achieving *rapprochement* between the two trends. His remedy for the split: experimental verification, involving the deduction of testable hypotheses from certain postulates which had been set forth at the meeting by Rollo May. What he was attempting was to bring under the covering statements of general laws certain phenomena which had been neglected by those of the objective trend, but, in his *rapprochement*, he played by the same rules of theory as those held by the objectivists. The point is simply that Rogers has never attempted a radical restructuring of the rules of explanation. He made the point quite clear in a paper which he presented at Rice University. In that address he states [22] that one must study the private worlds of inner personal meaning in order to discover the orderly and lawful relations there. Later on [23] he asserts that the existential area of human life can be dealt with in a thoroughly objective manner, "giving results which are replicable by any qualified scientist." [24] And still later, in a section which deals specifically with new developments,[25] in psychological theory, his concern is with

113

admitting to research and theory certain phenomena which have previously been excluded, but his assumption throughout is that deductive models are the appropriate tools for explaining human behavior. Those counselors who have looked to Rogers to humanize, to personalize, to de-scientize psychology may find in his techniques of therapy certain items of assistance, but to look to Rogers for a radically new, and more experientially based, conception of explanation is to be left wanting. At the point of explanation, Rogers, as a major representative of the third force in psychology, is at one with those who hold to a deductive pattern of explanation. One may conclude that, while the third force has begun moving toward a genuine concern with ordinary experience, it is still committed to the larger goals of the sociological-nomothetic orientation, attempting to encompass first-person experience within steno-language.

Explanation Criticized

Certain criticisms have already been made, primarily of those who have attempted to "humanize" explanation. It was noted that Louch, in his effort to radically restructure explanation, creates more difficulties than were had before by shifting explanation to a moral-appraisal operation. Barry and Wolf's attempt claims too much, epistemologically, and, after laying claim to a deductive form, they do not attend to the logical requirements of that form. And, Rogers does not attempt a restructuring of explanation at all.

Other specific criticisms have yet to be made. The most exact explanatory model discussed has been that of Hull and associates, yet they candidly admit that there are no rules for judging between contradicting postulates.[26] Their model is extremely exact with meaning precise and logic rigorous—so long as the postulates are agreed upon. When there is disagreement over the postulates or when two or more postulates are contradictory, the model breaks down. The problem is the same as that discussed in Chapter Two regarding exact meanings and usages of terms; the exactness of a word, or in this case an explanatory model, will always rely on a test which is not exact in the same sense as the word or model is said to be. At the point of postulates, Nagel's epistemic condition weakens still further the exactness claim of deductive explanation. As was discussed earlier, he says that all that is needed to establish the truth claim for the major premise is that there be no empirical evidence for regarding the premise as false while there must be some empirical evidence to support it. How much evidence is needed is not indicated, and how to handle two or more contradictory premises each having some support is not either. A last specific criticism is directed to Hempel's claim that general laws can be obtained for explaining historical phenomena. The ordinary experience of the people at a given time in the past cannot be discovered, except in certain limited ways, hence, historical explanation would always be incomplete. What universality can then be claimed for its laws? The laws might be true for a highly restricted type of discourse, but it would not permit a comprehensive history.

All three of these specific criticisms have been directed to the primary term in the deductive model of explanation, that is, to postulates, major premises, and general laws. If such primary terms could be had, then perhaps, deductive models would be appropriate conceptual schemes for explaining and predicting human behavior, but such terms always require epistemic conditions which simply cannot be met. As was pointed out in Chapter Three, there is no way to "get at" knowledge of the outer limits of an episode of experience; further, as was established in Chapter Five, any purported knowledge which goes beyond sensation and perception is nothing more than a construction. And some of our most sophisticated intellectual constructions have been explanatory models; the work of Hull and Nagel illustrates the point well.

Human experience overflows the categorical boundaries of explanatory models. If we could make ordinary experience orderly, sequential, and causally related in its parts, then explanatory models might "fit;" the postulates and general laws might actually tell us something about that experience. But the moment we recognize that the laws cannot meet their own epistemological claims, to use the words of Camus, "this world cracks and tumbles: an infinite number of shimmering fragments is offered to the understanding." [27] And even the philosopher of science is forced to discuss the world in metaphorical language. Steno-language, wherever it appears, in this case in explanatory models, is not adequate for either describing or explaining that which is ours in ordinary experience. If the diversity and contradictions and dilemmas of human experience overflow the boundaries of logical categories, then logic and explanatory models are to be ignored.

The psychologist, however, may be put off by this sort of talk. He persists with his assumption that, given adequate knowledge of environmental factors, conditioning schedules, resolution of conflicts at certain developmental stages, etc., he can explain and predict behavior. Several questions may be raised in respect to this contention. Is it ever possible to have this "adequate knowledge" of environmental factors, etc.? Even if it were possible to successfully identify all relevant environmental factors, what of the subject's perception of those factors? On what epistemological grounds can one assert that, at some specific point in time, we "know" the perceptions of another? And, what of the meanings assigned to these environmental factors by the subject? To argue that an adequate knowledge of past and present environmental factors will provide the basis for explaining current behavior and to avoid the problem of subjective meaning, one would, in addition to making the assumption of historical determinism, have to assume that environmental events possess meaning in themselves. Or, if one argues that the relevant data are not environmental factors but are patterns of conditioning and/or resolutions of psychoanalytic conflict stages—both of which would occur, according to respective theories, primarily at a level below that of awareness—the same questions hold. To put the matter in other terms, one may construct a mosaic of antecedent conditions, but the action taken in terms of this mosaic is not predictable for individuals in particular episodes of experience. There are necessary prerequisites for certain actions, of course, but one cannot claim knowledge of the sufficient conditions to bring about that action, for such a claim presumes knowledge of the parameters of that experience.

What explanatory models give us are after-the-fact symbolic patterns for organizing those aspects of the past which can be translated into the terms of the symbolic pattern; they are, thus, always closed systems. Understood as after-the-fact constructions, they may be useful for making orderly the way we talk about various domains, but, when used to explain and predict individual action, they become conceptual molds for freezing and distorting experience. Symbols take priority over body, and notions take priority over feelings; we, along with the rest of nature, are put at a distance so that we may be described, explained, and controlled. That which must be accomplished, therefore, is a rejoining of the constructions of thought to the experiential roots of that thought.

Explanation-as-Understanding

What is to be done, therefore, is to stop attempting to talk of the ordinary experience of the individual in terms of explanatory systems and to talk, instead, of understanding. As used here, the term *understanding* refers to a mode of individual organization of his reality, the organization arising out of the particular character of the multi-dimensional, simultaneous, field-likeness of his ordinary experience; that is, it arises out of the body-feels, as that term was used in Chapter Five, of the person, which then eventuate in communicable notions. While the ideal of explanation is mathematical (or other steno-language) exactness, the ideal of understanding is the perception of the expressive behavior of a single, other person.

This approach to the "explanation" of human behavior depends to a great extent on the pre-predicative, pre-logical body-feels of the individual, but this does not preclude the utilization of external explanatory models in the development of communicable notions. What it does do is to specify the starting point for the "explanation" and to limit strictly the validity which can be claimed for the model. As was pointed out earlier, since that which is most communicable is that which is least personal, no *a priori* model of explanation possesses value as a predictor, only after-the-fact value as one among several possible notions. Hence, what is being asserted is that explanatory models, particularly as they bear on the ordinary experience of the individual, possess no status prior to that ordinary experience and, further,

117

that their status possesses value only as after-the-fact modes for ordering into some communicable form the body-feels which were the origin of the original "problem." To illustrate briefly the effect of this conception in counseling, since it is the person as experiencing-body who determines the "validity" of his feeling/notion gestalts, it would be the client himself who determines the validity, for him, of any given test score, the appropriateness of any explanation given by the counselor, and the desirability of any prediction the counselor might make.

But we need to look in greater detail at this explanation-as-understanding to clarify its meaning and its bearings on counseling. Consider the following case of decision-making. A history professor in a small, southern university was offered the chairmanship of the history department in one of the "Big Ten" universities. The circumstances of the offer were such that his reply had to be given within forty-eight hours. The magnitude of the decision was immediately obvious. In accepting the offer he would be achieving the recognition desired by many; he would be making more money for himself and his family; and, he would be, in essence, defining himself as a rather different kind of man. In rejecting the offer he would not be expressing satisfaction with the status quo, but would be, in effect, opening the door for whatever future growth might be his at the southern university. He tried the introspection route but could come to no decision. He tried to be realistic about the matter, listing all conceivable pro's and con's, but no decision could be reached. A family conference was held in an attempt to be democratic about the matter. He tried the pragmatic anticipation of probable consequences, but that did not help. He even had a minister friend pray for him, but the answer was not revealed. The forty-eight hours were gone; he picked up the phone to place the call, still not knowing what he would say. He remembered having read somewhere about trusting the body, about letting the body control reason rather than the body being guided by rationality; so, at the moment the call went through, he opened his mouth intrigued at what would come out. He politely refused the offer. He reported to me that he had never felt such an intense sense of being at one with him-

118

self, and he and his wife went to bed where they played merrily for hours.

After the experience, my professor acquaintance began to read Sartre, the result being that he came to see his experience as an example of baseless choosing. When viewed in contrast to a nomothetic position, where decision-behavior is seen as subsumption under general laws, then most, if not all, decisions in life are baseless. But, when all "statements of self," including statements of choice, are seen as the bodying-forth of meaning, choices are not baseless. They are grounded in the decisive action of the individual, experiencing-body. Or, to put it in different terms, decisions are I-sentences, sentences of Type B. Even if the client, to put the matter back into the context of counseling, should accept a nomothetic explanation given by the counselor, he is saying "I accept the truth of that for my life." Even though the explanation may be couched in sentences of Type A, that is, objective steno-language, the appropriation of that explanation to the life of the client will always be in the form of Type B sentences. Which is to say, decision statements are always I-sentences. Hence, while decision-statements are not explicable in terms of general laws, on one hand, they are also not baseless, as certain existentialists assert, on the other; decision-statements, rather, are grounded in the I-sentences of the experiencing-body.

Explanation-as-understanding, then, refers to the building up of a mosaic of feelings for, appreciations of, notions of how, and communications of and about, but it will not provide an answer of "why." If one absolutely refuses to grant an approach to explanation which does not answer the why-question, a requirement in Nagel's model, for example, then, the only alternative is to accept the baselessness thesis. But, in ordinary experience, we do "explain" matters even if we do not know the why's. For example, if a baseball player is having difficulty with his batting, he does not go to the physicists to obtain a model of explanation; rather, he goes to an experienced coach who, in the mode of communication described in Chapter Three, draws parallels between his experience and that of the player. "You should make your swing like this" is much more explanatory than the laws of physics. The laws of physics are appropriate for

119

talking about certain kinds of statements and objects, but they have little to say to the domain of human action, of human experience.

Three concepts developed in earlier chapters—ordinary experience, the body as basis for existential communication, and feeling/notion gestalts of knowledge—have provided the basis for the criticisms of explanatory models made in this chapter and the basis for a new conception of explanation, namely, explanation-as-understanding. Nothing has been said about the counseling techniques which would be consistent with this conception of explanation, and no claim was made for the chapter to do such. But there are several techniques already available which would lend themselves to explanation-as-understanding. These are psychodrama, sensitivity training, dance-therapy, and *daseinanalyse*. The relationships between the techniques and the concept of explanation-as-understanding will need to be determined, but such inquiry goes beyond the scope of this work.

It has been demonstrated in this chapter that the models of explanation given to counselors simply are not appropriate for the experiential problems of their clients, that the decision statements of clients are always I-sentences, and, that, once having discarded nomothetic explanation, one does not have to accept the baselessness thesis of certain existentialists, but can talk, admittedly in a limited way, of explanation-as-understanding.

PART THREE

Chapter VII

EXISTENTIAL LANGUAGE AND EXISTENTIALISM

The Primacy of Education

This work began with an expression of concern regarding the extreme tension between education's complexity, on one hand, and the increasing dissatisfaction, disenchantment, even alienation of students and faculties, on the other. Later on, it was argued that the feelings of estrangement from ourselves and others, the inarticulable visceral dissonances, the clumsiness of our attempts at communication, the frightening awareness of the superficiality of most social intercourse, the sense of being lost in a rapidly changing world, the weariness of never being a significant factor in those changes—all testify to the sense of alienation produced by a society and education which thinks in the mode of and organizes itself according to the dictates of nomothetic reasoning. The work, thus, began with a rejection of what was called the sociological-nomothetic orientation of our society. This rejection included the standardized language, the claim of an objective knowledge, the assertion that human behavior can be explained in terms of general laws, and the top-down, line-staff organizational pattern of that orientation.

What has been suggested as an alternative is that education, instead of imposing on its own processes and structures steno-language, general laws and line-staff organizational charts, begin with the first-person experience, what has been called ordinary experience, of the individuals whose experience is being reconstructed, to use Dewey's term, through "formal" education. This is to say, that, since each person's education is his own, we should begin our study of education with language tools adequate for the task and then follow through the consequences of that new starting point, meaning that radical changes in our conceptions of knowledge, of explanation, and of organization will follow. What all this does is to force a redefinition of the term *education*, no longer in terms of structure, or of process, or of institution, or of organizational model, but in terms of the experiential world of the individuals whose lives are being changed.

Does the thrust of this work mean, therefore, that the special ideology of education is to be existentialism? Or, to put the question in other words, does the talk of education in the terms of existential language require an acceptance of existentialism of one's philosophy of education? Or simply, is the existential language of ordinary experience an existentialism? If one defines existentialism in the terms of Molina,[1] then the answer would be an absolute no. Molina takes the position that existentialism possesses a body of technical philosophy and that it is a significant philosophical movement capable of standing against older philosophical systems. He defines existentialism as "the systematic, often technical, exploration of the category of the individual." [2] If Molina would leave the matter at that level, there could be no great quarrel with the concept of ordinary experience, but he insists on making existentialism into a rational system itself; hence, if one accepts his definition, then one must say, no, the existential language of ordinary experience is not an existentialism. Hanna,[3] on the other hand, sees existentialism as not being just another rational system of philosophy, but as an orientation to an approach to, and a perspective on life which begins in the total, existing individual. Hanna's view is very similar to that of this work. But the question is not a primary one. That which is primary is education, defined as first person experience. One should, therefore, begin with what he has, not with rational systems, but with his own ordinary experience; he should work from that, letting the categorical labels be whatever you wish, for they too are only after-the-fact rationalizations. But let us not dismiss existentialism too quickly, for its goals appear to be very similar to those of this work, and its contributions to the philosophy of education have increased significantly in the last decade.

Existentialism in American Educational Philosophy [4]

A popular magazine [5] recently characterized contemporary American philosophy as a war between two opposing "schools" of thought, the Logicians and the Lotus-Eaters, the term *Logicians* referring to those philosophers who concern themselves primarily with the analysis of language; the term *Lotus-Eaters* referring to the existentialists. Although the article was a popular, non-technical rendering of the current situation, it was quite accurate. Concern with philosophic systems is, in the main, a dated concern. Present interests tend to follow one of two types of analysis: language analysis or phenomenological analysis of the category of existence. The case with general philosophy is also the case with educational philosophy. Since the late 1950's, there has been little concern with philosophic systems and their implications for education. Rather, the efforts of philosophers of education have revolved about the two types of analysis mentioned.

The parallel between general philosophy and educational philosophy continues further in that, with both, the analysis of language has attracted the interests and efforts of more philosophers than has existentialism. Existentialism, however, continues to gain attention in both spheres of philosophic activity. Educational philosophers, in particular, are forced to attend to the trenchant criticisms of the existentialists, for, by the very nature of their activity, philosophers of education are required to concern themselves with questions of particularly human concern, questions having to do with the development of specific human beings. The purpose of this section of the chapter, then, is to indicate something of the nature of the literature on existentialism in the journals and books of educational philosophy and to attempt an assessment of existentialism's influence on and status in American educational philosophy—all for the purpose of pointing toward the clarification of the relationship between the thrust of this work and existentialism.

Prior to the publication of Kneller's *Existentialism and Education* in 1958,[6] few articles had been written on the topic in the journals of educational philosophy. The publication of that volume, however, seemed to have opened the gates, and since then and with increasing frequency numerous articles and papers have been written. Only one other booklength treatment of the subject, that by Van Cleve Morris,[7] has been written since, but several leading textbooks in educational philosophy now have sections or chapters devoted to existentialism. What one finds in a survey of this body of literature are two approaches. The approach which is used more frequently involves an analysis of one or more aspects of existentialism to determine possible bearings on specific educational topics such as freedom, authority, subjective knowledge, and the objectification of students. The other approach has involved the setting forth of the philosophic positions and educational statements, if any, of certain existentialist philosophers.

The two philosophers of education who have done the most work in attempting to determine the bearings of existentialism on education have been George Kneller and Van Cleve Morris, to whom earlier references have been made. Although each draws from the works of Nietzsche, Kierkegaard, Heidegger, Marcel, Buber, and others, both rely primarily on the writings of Sartre. An interesting and somewhat amusing aside to this point was the exchange of articles between Vandenberg[8] and DeSoto[9] concerning Kneller's treatment of Heidegger in *Existentialism and Education*. Vandenberg argued that Kneller, by relying in the main on secondary sources had misconstrued the meaning of several of Heidegger's points, particularly Heidegger's notion of death. DeSoto replied by calling Vandenberg a "dedicated flawpicker." His reply, on a more serious note, pointed out that Kneller was attempting to demonstrate that in existentialism one could find adequate grounds for rejecting the usual concepts of social adjustment, replacing those concepts with an education which assists us in finding authentic meaning in life, in ourselves, and in our relations with others.

If one looks in Kneller for more definitive guidelines for educational practice than an emphasis on authenticity and the quest for personal meaning, he will be disappointed. True, Kneller does discuss the relation between the knower and the known; he does treat of the topics of death, anguish, and commitment and indicates the role of the teacher in bringing about awareness of these; he does point to the need of teachers to be authentic persons; and, he does em-

126

phasize the basic moral nature of an existentialist education. With the exception of some discussion of the place of literature and the arts in an existentialist curriculum, however, he does not tell the reader just what a curriculum, a course of study, or a school based on the "principles" of existentialism would look like.

Morris, in a text in the philosophy of education,[10] attempts to develop such specific guidelines. He says that the subject matters to be emphasized would be those which require individual choosing. He suggests art, ethics, moral philosophy, and religion as such subject matters. Socratic questioning is the teaching technique he suggests, and he points out that the entire process of education will be one of character education, since the primary goal of education will be that of responsible selfhood. In his later work, Morris [11] expands on what he calls the Socratic Paradigm as the teaching method most logically consistent with existentialism. Although there are empirically verifiable facts which can be "told," the personal appropriation of these to the life of each student involves the question of meaning which cannot be "told" but must be raised. Morris illustrates from art, literature, history, and religion just how this teaching by questioning might be done. The key feature in all of these is in the use of the "facts" of each. The information in each of these disciplines does not constitute the end of the instruction; rather, the information is used as a means of provoking the student to awareness and to making choices in respect to himself, the world, and other persons based on that awareness.

Kneller and Morris, working independently of each other, have exercised considerable influence among American philosophers of education by persistently raising the question, "Where are you other philosophers of education allowing, in your respective theories, for the subjectivity, for the authenticity of individual students?" Although Kneller has moved on to other topics of interest to him, Morris continues his investigations into the bearings of existentialism on education.

But Kneller and Morris have not been alone in their search for the meaning of existentialism for education. Several articles and papers have been directed to the same search. One article [12] and one paper [13] in particular, merit attention. In Bowers' article, he contends that if educational theorists are going to be taken seriously by the public, they will have to turn their attention to the problems of human existence. He points out that most theorists have already turned away from concerns with metaphysics but that, as an alternative, they have turned to pragmatism and social reconstructionism, both of which focus primarily on the needs of society. They ignore the existential components of man's nature where life's significant decisions are made. He further contends [14] that with our present system of education a student may go all through life on other people's facts and rules of conduct without ever formulating and expressing his own thoughts and feelings. By creating students who are self-reliant in the areas of ideas and values, the school accomplishes its task of making itself expendable.[15] With this conception of the task of the school, Bower may be proposing a solution to the problem found in the fact that, while schools must possess some institutional form, existentialists have either been indifferent to or somewhat antagonistic toward institutions in general.

The paper referred to is one by Troutner in which he sets forth five specifics which the educator can learn from the existential philosopher. In the first of these, Troutner points out that, although teachers have always complained of difficulty in understanding the desires, whims, etc., of their students, the mounting evidence indicates that the present generation of students "may take the prize" for being the most difficult to understand. It is at this point that he thinks existentialism can make a contribution in that the existentialists' analyses of the predicament of modern man, of the current human situation, provide new ways of viewing the stresses of the current generation of students. The second thing which educators can learn from existentialism, according to Troutner, is that educators have to too great extent treated students as objects to be manipulated rather than as subjects to be lived with. This point obviously is not new with Troutner, for both Kneller and Morris have criticized the objectification of students in American education. Troutner's third point has to do with the therapeutic value of existentialism on the personality of the teacher. By this he refers to the teacher's need for a keen awareness of his own values, attitudes, and of the pain associated with his own struggle to achieve authenticity. In the fourth point, he criticizes educators for being concerned more with transmitting specific facts than with developing each student's "completeness as a man." Troutner's last suggestion is directed to specialized areas in education such as educational psychology and counseling, areas which have traditionally dealt with students with little conception of what it means to be human. Insights from existential philosophy and phenomenology are bringing major changes in counseling, and he lends his support to this development.

In the beginning of this section a second approach in the literature on existentialism and education was mentioned, an approach that looked to particular existentialist writers. Over a period of five years, the journal *Educational Theory* published one such article each year. The series includes articles on Frankl,[16] Buber,[17] Camus,[18] Unamuno,[19] and Kierkegaard,[20] in that order.

Wirth, in the article on Frankl, briefly summarizes the main points of Frankl's thought and proceeds to indicate some of the possible outcomes in education if Frankl's emphasis on the development of responsible selfhood was also an emphasis of contemporary education. Winetrout points out that it is Buber who speaks most directly to the matter of teaching and to the matter of interpersonal relationships within the educational setting. The basic tenet of all such relationships, of course, is the I-Thou dialogue, and it is to this that Winetrout devotes most of his attention. In the article on Camus, Denton briefly explains the ontology of the absurd and the ethics of rebellion. From these two he derives three conclusions in respect to education. The first of these is that education, in its institutional form, can justify its existence only to the extent that it implements programs for the development of lucid—that is, moral—individuals. Since the school's rationale for existing is that it produce moral individuals, education is, in essence, a moral enterprise. His second conclusion follows from the first in that the primary purpose of education is not to develop rational men or social animals but, rather, to develop moral persons. The third conclusion is that all educational considerations are to be grounded in Camus' theory of man rather than in assertions about the nature of society, or of history, or of the universe, or of God. The article on Unamuno deals primarily with Unamuno's statement regarding his role as provocateur in his teaching and his statements on the nature of knowledge and truth. Hill's article on Kierkegaard is an attempt to clarify what Hill perceives as being misconceptions of Kierkegaard in the literature of educational philosophy. After a brief biographical note, he discusses Kierkegaard's philosophic method, Kierkegaard's criticism's of Hegel's conceptions of society, Kierkegaard's psychology, and his political position. Because of the stated purpose of the article, to clarify misconceptions in the literature, Hill makes no attempt in the essay to find any "implications" for education.

To this point, I have attempted to indicate the nature of the literature which has dealt with existentialism and its possible effects in education. An assessment of the influence and status of existentialism in American educational philosophy is a much more difficult task. Certain observations, in addition to the fact of the increasing number of articles on the topic, can be made which will assist in the assessment.

Existentialism is an extremely popular topic among undergraduates on American college and university campuses. Students have become quite involved with the writings of such thinkers as Jean-Paul Sartre and Albert Camus. On almost any campus, one can start an immediate debate over the relative merits of these and other writers. This enthusiasm has spilled over into education courses, particularly those labelled philosophy of education and foundations of education. Professors, on more than one occasion, have been forced to "catch up" with their students by the insistent questioning of those students. Several texts in philosophy of education, by now including sections or chapters on existentialism, have given students additional opportunity to raise such questions. And a few universities, because of the orientations of the professors involved, actively encourage students in education to grapple with the topics and questions of existentialism.

A major problem, however, militates against existentialism's having a great deal of influence on educational practice. Although it does treat of topics generally overlooked in educational thought—subjectivity, self-identification, and metaphysical anxiety, for example—few guides for action have been derived. What would a curriculum based on existentialism consist of? In what ways would the behavior of an "existentialist teacher" differ from any other teacher? Would an "existentialist administrator" operate in ways different from any other? Is the very existence of the school as an institution of society consistent with existentialism's general lack of concern with and for institutions? These and other similar questions have yet to be answered. True, courses of action have been suggested. Several of these have been mentioned. But, thus far, the suggested courses of action have been without sufficient force of argument to convince most professors of educational administration and professors of teacher education.

Philosophically, there is yet another major difficulty. Existentialism has been dealt with as though it were another rational system, yielding implications for education. The most glaring example of this is that of Morris who, in his first work,[21] attempts to treat existentialism in the same long breath with Idealism, Realism, Neo-Thomism, and Experimentalism. He sets up ontological statements and, in an extremely loose fashion, "derives" educational implications from those statements.[22] In a similar manner, he sets up epistemological statements of existentialism and "derives" implications for educational method from those.[23] Continuing his rational, deductive approach to the task, he treats axiological statements the same way.[24] As if to make certain that no one would misunderstand his thinking, he carefully develops a two-page "Schematic Summary of Views" which presents philosophic statement with the direct educational implication from each of the philosophic systems he has discussed in the book. And, in that schematic summary as elsewhere in the work, existentialism is handled in the same manner as any other rational system. In *Existentialism in Education,* his later work which was referred to earlier, Morris' thinking has not changed. The first part of the book is devoted to explanation of existential philosophy; the second, to educational theory; and, the third, to an existentialist pedagogy. And each section is supposedly derived from the preceding one in a deductive fashion.

This same misconception of existentialism is also found in the latest edition of one of the most well-known works in philosophy of education. In that work,[25] Butler adds a section on existentialism, treating it as he had earlier treated other rational philosophies, that is, by setting forth their major covering statements and, then, deriving, also in an extremely loose fashion, implications for educational theory and practice from those general statements. Even Molina, who conceives of existentialism as a rational philosophy, does not attempt to derive specific statements of action. The fallacy is not only in treating of existentialism as though it were but another system offering alternative answers to all the traditional questions, but is also in the looking to general laws, postulates, major premises, etc., for something to transfer over onto, to impose on education, rather than beginning with that which is given in the experience of education itself. Existentialism, therefore, is not the primary question, concern, or focus. Education is. To the extent that existentialism contributes to an understanding of this experience, it is consistent with the thesis of this work. To the extent that it is, or has been used as, a rational deductive system of thought, it is irrelevant and contradictory to the task of this work. Again, existentialism is not primary; education is.

Toward a Philosophy of 'Education'

All of this—the criticisms of those matters subsumed under the term *sociological-nomothetic* and the criticisms of existentialism in educational philosophy—points toward a new conception of philosophy of education. Different conceptions of the term are numerous, and it is an old game to construct additional ones. It is possible, however, to sort out the different senses in which the term has been used to determine what, if anything, has been left out of consideration. Most analyses of this type have stopped short of this purpose, being content to merely catalogue uses of the term. A well-known analysis of this type is that of Smith who finds four senses of the term *philosophy of education*. Smith [26] classifies the four senses under the headings of philosophy *and* education, philosophy *in* education, philosophy *for* education, and philosophy *of* education. The first of these, philosophy *and* education, is the sense in which a specific philosophy of education is a derivative of some general philosophy. The second, philosophy *in* education, is a much less systematic sense of the term, referring, not to a general philosophy, but to a process of analyzing various case studies with a variety of philosophic methods. Philosophy *for* education, the third sense according to Smith's classification, consists of a set of prescriptive proposals for education; that is, philosophy for education is the use of philosophy in education to bring about a commonality of belief regarding certain educational issues. The fourth sense, philosophy *of* education, is that conception of educational philosophy which models somewhat loosely after philosophy of science, focusing not so much on implications for educational practice as on the discipline of philosophy of education itself.

Smith's analysis is of assistance at this point, for it indicates clearly, though by indirection, that which has been left out of consideration. The first and third of his classes are systematic-deductively focused; the second is focused on cases and issues; and, the fourth is concerned primarily with method and approach. No one of these is focused on the experience of education of the individual. It is that which has been left out of consideration. In fact, if we accept literally the definition of education as first-person experience, then it can be said that philosophy *and, in, for* and *of* education has not really been about education at all. These conceptions of philosophy of education do contribute to the analysis and explanation of education as institution, of education as structure and process, of education as method. But another conception is required if we are to speak meaningfully of the individual persons in that institution.

Thus, a redefinition of the term *philosophy of education* is called for. Philosophy of education will no longer be the philosophy of language with focus on educational discourse, will no longer be the philosophy of metaphysics with implications for education, will no longer be the philosophy of science with theoretical models for education. With education defined as first-person experience, philosophy of education becomes the philosophy of 'education' with its own unique "area" of inquiry, that is, the educational experience of the individual. The point of origin of the inquiry, the methods of the inquiry, and the language and conceptual tools for the inquiry will be those which have been set forth in this work.

Chapter VIII

CONCLUDING NOTES

The Thesis Restated

This work has been built upon three assertions: that the major educational problems of this era are the results of our talking of education in sociological-nomothetic terms, that education is ultimately first-person experience, and that the language and conceptual tools for talking of education as first-person experience are those referred to in this work as existential language. That the consequences of conceiving of education in this radically different manner are quite extensive was noted in the first chapter, but the work here has been limited to the setting forth of the grounds for the assertions and the language and conceptual tools required by this conception of education. A more detailed examination of the consequences in respect to knowledge and explanation has been made, and the relationship of existential language and existentialism in education has also been examined. This concluding chapter will attempt no summary of what has been said, but will treat briefly of why language, knowledge, and explanation have been selected for special attention and, then, will suggest possible consequences in two areas which are of particular relevance to the current dissatisfaction within and without educational institutions, namely, organization and the so-called generation gap.

Language, Knowledge, and Explanation

The author has not been alone in his concern with the depersonalized nature of current education. A few voices have been raised from the ranks of curriculum and instruction specialists; a few theorists in educational administra-

134

tion have attempted to replace the notion of "scientific" administration with a "clinical" conception;[1] and, numerous references have already been made to the concern held by those in the so-called third force in psychology and counseling. But, until certain basic philosophic issues—language, knowledge, and explanation—have been faced and grappled with and resolved, the suggestions of the concerned will consist of window dressing and little more, for new conceptions of the function of teachers will be meaningless as long as they are discussed in isolation from the dehumanizing nature of present educational organization; new proposals for curriculum reorganization and teaching method will prove no more "human" than the old if considered without regard for the epistemological assumptions underlying the proposed curricula and methods; and, when new teaching methods are proposed without considering the nature of explanation, that which the method is supposed to do, superior levels of superficiality of thought will have been demonstrated. All of this is not to say that no one else has been aware of the necessity of including consideration of philosophic issues in the development of new proposals, but it is to say that attempts to "humanize" curriculum, method, counseling, etc., have, in the main, been more involved with techniques and immediate effects than with the task of radically restructuring the basic philosophic principles themselves.

Philosophers of education have been quite concerned with the problems of language, knowledge, and explanation, but, with few exceptions, their work has been limited to a copying of the work of Anglo-American philosophers. And, as has been pointed out, the exceptions have attempted to derive, in a deductive manner, guidelines from existential-phenomenological philosophy. No one, however, has begun with a radical conception of education and then treated the problems of language, knowledge, and explanation in terms of that conception. These problems are at the heart of philosophy, but they are just as well at the heart of education. Hence, this work has focused on these three major problems in the process of education from the perspective of education defined as first-person experience.

A giant heresy was set forth in chapters five and six, namely, that conceptions of knowledge and explanation, to be genuinely human, must be grounded in the feeling-states of individual persons. It is important that that heresy also be generalized to organizational theory. It is perhaps of even more importance that organizational theory be grounded in the feeling-states of individuals, for, while individuals may live their lives ignorant of epistemology and philosophy of science, they would be hard put indeed to live their lives ignorant of organizations. And, while school and university administrators may remain indifferent to the intellectual games which teachers and professors may play with epistemology and explanation, they cannot long remain indifferent to a radically different conception of organization itself. The purpose of this book has been to begin our inquiry at the ordinary experience of the individuals in the educative process and to let the chips fall where they will. If, by beginning the inquiry at that point, it is determined that hierarchical administration and top-down organizational charts must be done away with, then do away with them; the outcome may be less efficient and less exact, but it will be more human, more relevant.

To talk this way is, of course, to talk of matters for which steno-language has no capability. What, specifically then, can steno-language account for in respect to organization, and what can it not? With the terms of steno-language, one can speak of organizational structure and of organizational processes, both of which can be analyzed into highly specific, quantitative units, and the referents can be indicated with high degrees of precision. But when one asks about the vitality, the élan, the quality of the organization, steno-language becomes inadequate. When asked of such matters, the administrator will translate the question into terms of morale, which he defines quantitatively. He will tell you how long his employees (professors) remain with the company (university) ; he will tell you of the elaborate feedback system built into the structure and processes of the organization by his scientific management consultants. The attempts in the last decade to develop programs of quality education have produced even greater alienation on the part of faculty and students, for educational administrators have attempted to consider quality in the terms of steno-language. To design "quality" programs in behavioristic terms and to analyze the results in quantitative terms is to simply negate the goal of quality, is to simply kill the soul.

And what do I mean by the term *soul?* With the term *soul* I am referring to such feeling-personal matters as élan, spontaneity, vitality, pride, warmth, compassion, and concern. I am not using the term as a way of introducing, in the last chapter, a Platonic or any other metaphysical conception of soul; rather, I am using the term in the same sense in which it is used by Negro musicians and by others who have experienced deeply the pains, the frustrations, the joys, the frequent hopelessness—in short, the conditions of human existence. The black musician has no special corner on the term, for, in varying ways, we all have shared in the conditions of human existence. In varying ways, we have shaken our fists at the rigidity of the structures of our society, at the stereotyped and bureaucratic processes of those structures. To paraphrase Russell,[2] the organization does not feel pleasure and pain; it has no hopes and fears. And what we think of as its purpose are really the purposes of individuals who direct it. Glorification of the organization turns out to be, in fact, glorification of an administrative minority; dominance by the organization turns out, in fact, to be dominancy by an administrative minority. When men in control of organizations begin to think too abstractly, begin to reify their organizational charts, they begin to fit men to systems rather than systems to men. To quote Russell, "No democrat can tolerate such a fundamentally unjust theory." When the Budapest blacksmith[3] was asked what he was fighting for, he did not refer directly to the structures and processes of governmental organization, but to the fact that no one would listen to him. When the dictator in Camus' play *State of Siege*[4] bragged that he had achieved complete control of the state, his secretary startled him by saying that there was one thing he could never completely control: the people's pride. He could not understand what she was saying. When an American presidential candidate said, "These people are anarchists and nihilists who believe in nothing," the students responded, "You wouldn't understand." When the students who campaigned for the presidential nomination

137

of Senator Eugene McCarthy were asked what they meant when they said that the establishment did not know what was happening, they had almost insurmountable difficulty in answering. For what was happening was the loss of soul, of feeling, of concern, of warmth, of compassion from the political system—matters which the politician, who has been conditioned to think of organization only in terms of structure and process, could not grasp. Even the "third force" psychologists, who do recognize that the qualitative aspects of human existence are missing in our attempts to organize that existence, have missed the point. S. Jourard, for example, in his *The Transparent Self*,[5] introduces the use of the term *soul* but then equates it with the term *self* after defining self in social-process terms, which, of course, puts him right back where he began. Soul, then, is the missing term in our conceptions of organization. Steno-language provides the conceptual tools for talking of structure and process, but not for talking of soul.

But that concluding sentence requires more. It requires that a more careful analysis of the relationship between steno-language and organization be made. To talk of the relationships among people with the terms of steno-language is to characterize those relationships as being linear in order, reductionistic in description, exact in respect to function, objective in respect to referents, and scientific in its claims. An analysis of the organizational models and charts of most industries and universities will demonstrate clearly the dominance of these characteristics. But to talk of organization with steno-language one must speak with even greater precision; specifically, what is the basic unit of the steno-language of organization? Put simply, it is the role. The role can be identified with exactness, is objective in respect to its referents, can be analyzed in linear and curvilinear terms in its relation to other roles, is itself a reductionistic unit, and, to the satisfaction of the sociologists, meets the test of being a scientific unit of investigation.

I am not implying that the role is a simplistic concept. Parsons and Shils [6] have made the point quite clear that action in a network of relationships entails the personality variables of the actors. Yet, they negate their own point by

138

making the normative position in the field of relationships (the role) the basic conceptual unit in an organization. Thus, on one hand, they have admitted that action must include the personalities of actors, while, on the other, they exclude individual personality variables from their theory. Why? I think the answer is obvious. Given the objective nature of steno-language, one cannot construct a theory of organization, or a theory of anything, which will be consistent with the presuppositions of steno-language and, at the same time, account for, open the door to, the idiographic, simultaneous, protean characteristics of individual persons in the operation. The role, therefore, defined as a normative position in a field, becomes the basic unit in the construction of organizational theory.

The organization, described and explained with the terms of steno-language, becomes an impersonal structure, an objective, external force of evaluation, with efficiency, exactness, and economy being its hallmarks.[7] The ordinary experience of the individual ceases to be a significant factor. Individuals come into the organization, experience their frustrations and delights, their dreams and their failures, and then go, but the organization lives on. Individual lives have no meaning save that which is given by their relationship to the organization. Within the organization, the values of the individual must be subordinated to those of the organization, for the very definition of role is that of evaluation. In fact, according to Parsons and Shils,[8] if the organizational values are not shared, there is no organization. The goal of this dominance of organizational over individual values is "conflictless action on the part of the several actors."[9] In such an arrangement, the dramatic-dialectic of dialogue is dead. But, the organization lives. There is, of course, no organization without people, but, given the steno-language with which we talk about organizations, they must be designed in such a way as to be independent of the individuals who constitute the operation at any given moment in time.

Such design produces two opposite effects, a convergence toward and an alienation from the organization. The convergence is one of thinking alike in respect to the organization itself and of agreeing on the locus of value;

that is to say, the locus of value is the organization rather than the particular persons. This convergence permits a centralization of control which may be very impersonal, even inhuman, but which is very precise, orderly, and efficient. But this same convergence finds its opposite effect in alienation on the part of the individuals in the organization, for the individuals lose sight of, are no longer personally involved with, the product, the structure of the organization inhibits personal involvement with either the organization itself or with the management (administration), and the requirement of specification and order precludes spontaneity and creative efforts which do not conform to departmental lines. To illustrate from the university scene, this alienation is evidenced by students in their complaints regarding the impersonalization, the mass-production nature of their education and by professors who have simply "dropped out" of the university-organizational game by identifying primarily with a particular discipline rather than with a particular university; thus, the increasing mobility of top-level professors who are more concerned with having the freedom to conduct their inquiry as they choose than with more traditional organizational "gifts" such as tenure.

Another effect of organizations designed in terms of steno-language and one which has been studied in detail by sociologists is that of informal power "structures" which develop among the members of an organization but which are not part of the design of the organization. Since organizational design can say little, if anything, about persons, informal arrangements will develop, for the simple reason that the life forces, the spontaneity, the élan, the ordinary experience of persons overflow the bounds of any organizational chart. To summarize to this point, to discuss organization in the terms of steno-language is to discuss it in terms of task segmentation, differential status, commonality of values, and extrinsic hierarchical control.

To talk of organization with the terms of existential language would not be to immediately negate, throw out, all organizational theory, but would be to question the status of such theory. Existential language consists of the presuppositions, concepts, and tools for talking of first-person experience and, further, for restructuring our notions of theory itself, restructuring always with reference to the ordinary experience of individuals. The status of theory is that of a notion, as that term was defined in Chapter Five, which is grounded in the feelings of individuals. When organizational theory ignores its feeling-origins, alienation occurs, and the members of the organization begin to refer to the organization as "they." At that moment, the organization ceases to possess what Russell calls "psychological reality." [10] At that moment, the individuals within the organization cease identifying with the organization, informal power structures develop, and some members "drop out." From that moment, administrators become more and more concerned with formalizing the procedures of the organization and individual members become known as *personnel*.

I am both amused and depressed when I see teachers distressed because certain students do not perform various tasks as anticipated. Terms such as unmotivated, unappreciative, etc., are used to describe the students. I react in a similar fashion to political leaders who, when they do not find significant numbers of the population responding to their programs as they anticipated, use the above terms plus ones such as lawless, disorderly, etc. Or, when administrators find teachers not "appreciating" what they do on the teachers' behalf, I laugh, for, when the goals, desires, and programs of the organization cease to be the goals and desires of the individual members, the leaders in the organization appear as ludicrous as the naked king without a kingdom.

What all of this points to is simply that an organizational theory or model has no more status than an epistemological-notion or an explanatory one. Or, to put the point in other terms, organizations have tool value only and no more status than an *ad hoc* committee. As long as they are in coherence with the actual people involved, they have "real" status; when they lose existential contact with the actual people involved, they remain only "paper tigers." What must be remembered is that organizations are language derivatives, not metaphysical derivatives, and language is an individual body derivative. Strip organizations of their origins (experiencing-bodies), and dehumanization

141

occurs; organizations become the repressive forces of society rather than life facilitating ones. In the case of schools, the effects can be especially devastating, for it is the very young who are being processed through and by such an organization.

New York City's attempt to "bring theatre to the people" may assist in clarifying the use of existential language in talking of organization. Several efforts were made, some by the city itself and some by certain theatre groups, to take theatre to the ghettoes, but the approaches were essentially the same. A pre-determined organization of events and activities and a pre-determined list of plays were brought to certain ghetto sections of the city. All met with failure, even though the efforts were publicly supported by a popular mayor. One director, however, has been able to "make contact" with the people of those sections; that man, Enrique Vargas. Vargas insists that his actors be well trained but, also, that they be attuned to the moods, movements, rhythms of the people. He sends them to services at storefront churches; he sends them on night strolls through the streets of the sections; he insists that they immerse themselves in the feeling-states of the people. And, as a result, of all the efforts attempted, his has been the only one to succeed with the people of the ghettoes. When asked what the first step is in organizing people for such a theatrical effort, he set forth a rule so simple as to be left out of organizational theory and models. "Find the simple way which won't turn people off." [11]

That's the starting point for any organizational effort, yet, in its simplicity, it is complex, for one of its basic terms, "turn people off," is an existential term. Vargas has demonstrated the point well that organizations to be meaningful must be grounded in the ordinary experience of individuals and talked about in terms appropriate to that experience. All of this would suggest that to talk of organization with the existential language of our ordinary experience would be to talk of autonomous groups, spontaneous order, workers' and students' and faculties' control, and the principle of federation. No such organization will not be as exact, as orderly, as efficient as that constructed with the terms of steno-language, but, to paraphrase

Camus,[12] when administrators succeed in molding the world according to their organizational laws, it will not prove quantity to be king, but that this world is hell.

Implied in this discussion of ordinary experience and organization is a thesis, the development of which goes beyond the scope of this work, but which does deserve to be identified and made explicit. That thesis is that the structure of language becomes the structure of organization. This thesis is, of course, part of the larger thesis that the structure and terms of language become the structure and terms of our conceptions of the world. This larger thesis, as expressed in the works of Benjamin Whorf and others, is quite familiar, but the focusing of that thesis specifically on organization is not. The delimiting of the larger thesis to organization, however, should not provoke surprise, for organization is itself one expression of our world, and, as such, it is limited to its means of expression. Thus, if we change the nature of expression, we also change the nature of organization. Within the boundaries of steno-language, changes may be made by shifting from atomistic to molar units of consideration, by attending to content rather than structure, and by substituting a process conception of nouns for a static one. But if an even more radical change is made in expression, such as going beyond the boundaries of steno-language to existential language, even greater changes will take place in our conceptions and theories of organization.

Ordinary Experience and the "Generation Gap"

Much has been written about the so-called generation gap of our day. Laymen, as well as social and behavioral scientists of all types, have gotten in on the act. Some dismiss it; some argue that there has always been a generation gap; others argue that the phenomenon of our day is different both in degree and kind from anything we have seen before. All of those, however, who assert the reality of the gap agree that in one way or another a breakdown of communication is involved. The concept of communication set forth in this work and the larger concept of existential language should provide assistance in a greater understanding of the phenomenon. In fact, one way to look

143

at the generation gap is to see it as the shift from categorical thinking with its steno-language to ordinary experience with its existential language. It is the purpose of this section to explore that possibility.

The generation gap, defined as the shift from categorical thinking to ordinary experience, is the shift from an emphasis on the rational to an emphasis on the intuitive, from a primary concern with means to a primary concern with ends, from a goal of quantification to an awareness of quality, of soul, from the use of the present for future purposes to an indulgence in and appreciation for the present, and from the interpreting of the present with concepts of the past to a viewing of the present in terms of the present. The shift may also be expressed with Camus' differentiation between "to go for a swim" and "to indulge in a swim." [13] The view held by the older side of the generation gap (or those referred to in the Broadway musical *Hair* as Mr. 1948's) would be that of the first term. "To go for a swim" indicates a planned, sequential order and the "means" status of swimming; "to indulge in a swim," on the other hand, indicates a multi-dimensional, all-at-onceness of experience and a multi-sensuous involvement which is an end in itself. It is the difference between categorical thinking and ordinary experience.

The gap between the generations is also created by the respective language modes of categorical thinking and ordinary experience. For steno-language, communication is linear and utilitarian; for existential language, communication is the sense of having-in-common which is transmitted metaphorically, that is, by drawing parallels between and among our experiences. When Mr. 1948 speaks of the Vietnam conflict, for example, he speaks in terms of abstract causes, such as freedom and democracy and national interest and economic stability. When the young talk of the same conflict, it is in terms of an identification with the ordinary experience of the Vietnamese people to the extent that parallels of experience can be drawn. And, underscoring McLuhan's thesis, television now makes such parallels possible. No, Mr. 1948 does not understand what is happening for he is talking with the terms of steno-language; he is interpreting the present with concepts from the past; and, he values the present only in utilitarian ways.

144

As a result of his not understanding, he attempts to set up whatever mechanisms are necessary for keeping experience within the boundaries of his categories. That which he cannot classify, he condemns. And, his condemnation takes forms ranging from mild admonishments to Selective Service repressions to police brutality to a more generalized cry for law and order. Educational institutions, being administered by Mr. 1948's, are active agents in the condemnation process. The "well-adjusted" student who succeeds in our educational institutions is the one who dresses as he is told, grooms as he is told, thinks as he is told, and feels the feelings which are acceptable. He succeeds, for he acts in ways which are understandable to the older generation; that is, he fits the predetermined categories of the older generation. Should he dress as he chooses, or groom as he pleases, or think divergently, or express what he genuinely feels, he would most likely be, in one manner or another, forced out of the institution. When we have the ordinary experience of individuals dominated by rational categories instead of ordinary experience expressing itself with reason, we create a world which is anti-life, in which the individual must submit to the needs of top-down organization, must postpone the moment for some future utility, futility.

Conclusion

This chapter of concluding notes has attempted to make clear the most general thrust of this work, not by summarizing the content of earlier chapters, but by continuing the exploration of the thesis through projecting that thesis into two larger domains, one being organization and the other being a particular, current social problem. The treatments of these two have been suggestive only. More detailed treatments have been made of certain topics which are specifically philosophical. Yet, even those have not been exhaustive and final, for a work on ordinary experience can make no claim of being final without denying its own premises.

NOTES

Chapter I

1. Certain movements in contemporary theatre also suggest the changes that must take place in philosophy of education if education is not to be left by the wayside of history as an institutional relic. When the character in the Broadway musical *Hair* says to the academicians, "Up your curriculum" he was speaking, I think, for a large number of the most aware, intelligent adults of our day.

2. B. F. Skinner (New York: Appleton-Century-Crofts, 1968).

3. E. Durkheim, *The Elementary Forms of the Religious Life* (New York: Collier Books, 1961), p. 32.

4. J. Cohen, *Humanistic Psychology* (New York: Collier Books, 1962), p. 33.

5. Durkheim, *op. cit.*, pp. 31 ff.

6. E. Tiryakian, *Sociologism and Existentialism* (Englewood Cliffs, N.J.: Prentice Hall, Inc., 1962), p. 13.

7. M. Bressler, "The Conventional Wisdom of Education and Sociology," in *Sociology and Contemporary Education*, edited by C. Page (New York: Random House, 1963-64), pp. 87-88.

8. J. Mora, *Man at the Crossroads* (Boston: Beacon Press, 1957), p. 202.

9. R. Stalcup, *Sociology and Education* (Columbus: Charles E. Merrill, 1968), pp. 61-63.

10. In P. Thévenaz, *What is Phenomenology?* (Chicago: Quadrangle Books, 1962), p. 19.

11. G. Schrader, *Existential Philosophers: Kierkegaard to Merleau-Ponty* (New York: McGraw-Hill, 1967), p. 30.

12. Edmund Husserl, trans. by W. R. Boyce Gibson (New York. Macmillan Co., 1931).

13. D. Cairns, "Phenomenology," *History of Philosophical Systems*, edited by V. Ferm (Paterson, N.J.: Littlefield, Adams and Co., 1961), pp. 355-359.

14. *Ibid.*, pp. 355-356.

15. D. Snygg and A. Combs, *Individual Behavior* (New York: Harper and Row, 1949).

16. C. Beck, *Philosophical Foundations of Guidance* (Englewood Cliffs, N.J.: Prentice-Hall, 1963), pp. 66-76.

17. S. Tenenbaum, "Implications of a Phenomenological Approach to Education," *Educational Theory*, Vol. 17 (October 1967), 343-352.

18. In Thévenaz, *op. cit.*, p. 25.

19. E. Kaelin, *An Existentialist Aesthetic* (Madison: The University of Wisconsin Press, 1966), p. 230.

20. M. McLuhan, *The Gutenberg Galaxy* (Toronto: University of Toronto Press, 1962), p. 278.

21. J. Culkin, "A Schoolman's Guide to Marshall McLuhan," *Saturday Review*, (March 18, 1967), 70-71.

22. J. Saunders and D. Henze, *The Private-Language Problem* (New York: Random House, 1967), pp. 12-24.

23. *Ibid.*, p. 187.

24. S. Kierkegaard, *The Point of View of my Work as an Author* (New York: Harper Torchbooks, 1962), p. 128.

25. N. Chiaromonte, "Albert Camus," *New Republic*, CXIV (April 29, 1946), 632.

26. P. Goodman, "Freedom and Learning: The Need for Choice," *Saturday Review* (May 18, 1968), 73-75.

27. The term *referential theory* is used here in a very broad sense to include not only approaches such as that of Ayer but also those of the ordinary language analysts.

Chapter II

1. E. Best, "The Suppressed Premiss in Educational Psychology," in *Psychological Concepts in Education*, edited by B. Komisar and C. Macmillan (Chicago: Rand McNally, 1967), pp. 1-13.

2. R. Mosier, "From Inquiry Logic to Symbolic Logic," *Educational Theory*, Vol. 18 (Winter 1968), 32-38.

3. A. Korzybski, *Science and Sanity* (Lancaster, Penna.: The Science Press Printing Co., 1933).

4. S. Hayakawa, *Language in Thought and Action* (New York: Harcourt Brace, 1949).

5. C. Morris, *Signs, Language and Behavior* (Englewood Cliffs, N.J.: Prentice-Hall, 1946).

6. A. Ayer, *Language, Truth and Logic* (New York: Dover Publications, [n.d.]).

7. *Ibid.*, pp. 134-138.

8. *Ibid.*, p. 137.

9. *Ibid.*, pp. 138-146.

10. I. Scheffler, *The Language of Education* (Springfield, Ill.: Charles C. Thomas, 1960), pp. 76-101.

11. J. Roland, "On the Reduction of 'Knowing That' to 'Knowing How,' " in *Language and Concepts in Education*, edited by B. Smith and R. Ennis (Chicago: Rand McNally, 1961), pp. 59-71.

12. R. Peters, "The Concept of Character," in Komisar and Macmillan, *op. cit.*, pp. 72-82.

13. B. Komisar and J. Coombs, "The Concept of Equality in Education," *Studies in Philosophy and Education*, III (Fall 1964), 223-244.

14. P. Wheelwright, *Metaphor and Reality* (Bloomington: Indiana University Press, 1962), pp. 33-38 and 94. See also his *The Burning Foundation/A Study in the Language of Symbolism* (Bloomington: Indiana University Press, 1954), pp. 25-29 and 55-59.

15. This use of the term *steno-language* is very similar to Koestenbaum's use of the term *precise-fact*. Precise facts, says Koestenbaum, "are facts that can be described more or less unambiguously, that can be measured or compared to some standard, that can be symbolized or expressed numerically, that are public, etc." P. Koestenbaum, "Phenomenological Foundations for the Behavioral Sciences: The Nature of Facts," *Journal of Existentialism*, VI (Spring 1966), 315. Although his term *precise-fact* is quite relevant to the interests at this point, an explanation of his theory of facts would lead us too far afield.

16. G. Schrader, *Existential Philosophers: Kierkegaard to Merleau-Ponty* (New York: McGraw-Hill, 1967), p. 44.

17. W. Quine, "Ontological Relativity," *The Journal of Philosophy*, LXV (April 4, 1968), 188-193.

18. M. Polanyi, *Personal Knowledge* (New York: Harper Torchbooks, 1964), pp. 94-95.

19. F. Waismann, "Verifiability," in *Logic and Language*, edited by A. Flew (New York: Doubleday Anchor Books, 1965), pp. 125-126.

20. Polanyi, *op. cit.*, p. 251.

21. Cited in W. Frankena, *Philosophy of Education* (New York: Macmillan, 1965) p. 14.

22. J. Soltis, *An Introduction to the Analysis of Educational Concepts* (Reading, Massachusetts: Addison-Wesley, 1968), p. xi.

23. F. Waismann, "Language Strata," in Flew, *op. cit.*, p. 241.

Chapter III

1. S. Langer, *Mind: An Essay on Human Feeling*, Vol. I (Baltimore: The Johns Hopkins Press, 1967), p. 155.

2. K. Harries, "Irrationalism and Cartesian Method," *Journal of Existentialism*, VI (Spring 1966), 295.

3. M. McLuhan, *The Gutenberg Galaxy* (Toronto: University of Toronto Press, 1962), p. 267.

4. Langer, *op. cit.*, p. 175.
5. W. Köhler, *Dynamics in Psychology* (New York: Liveright, 1940), p. 55.
6. K. Lewin, *Principles of Topological Psychology* (New York: McGraw-Hill, 1936), p. 12.
7. C. Hall and G. Lindzey, *Theories of Personality* (New York: John Wiley & Sons, 1957), p. 207.
8. Cited in W. Ellis, *A Source Book of Gestalt Psychology* (New York: The Humanities Press, 1950), p. 2.
9. A. Watts, *The Book* (New York: Pantheon Books, 1966), pp. 52-53.
10. *Ibid.*, p. 117.
11. P. Wheelwright, *Metaphor and Reality* (Bloomington: Indiana University Press, 1962), p. 166.
12. McLuhan, *op. cit.*, p. 14.
13. M. McLuhan and Q. Fiore, *The Medium is the Massage* (New York: Bantam Books, 1967), pp. 92-93.
14. Wheelwright, *op. cit.*, pp. 50-52.
15. S. Langer, *Philosophy in a New Key* (New York: New American Library, 1948), pp. 39-54.
16. Lewin, *op. cit.*, pp. 166-168.
17. A. Borgmann, "Language in Heidegger's Philosophy," *Journal of Existentialism*, VII (Winter 1966/67), 161-180.
18. *Ibid.*, p. 165.
19. M. Cohen and E. Nagel, *An Introduction to Logic and Scientific Method* (New York: Harcourt, Brace and Company, 1934), p. 139.
20. E. Madden, *Philosophical Problems of Psychology* (New York: The Odyssey Press, 1962), p. 31.
21. *Ibid.*, pp. 38-43.

Chapter IV

1. G. Kneller, *Logic and Language of Education* (New York: John Wiley & Sons, 1966), pp. 170-171.
2. M. McLuhan, *The Gutenberg Galaxy* (Toronto: University of Toronto Press, 1962), p. 265.
3. *Ibid.*, p. 25.
4. N. Brown, *Life Against Death* (Middletown, Conn.: Wesleyan University Press, 1959), p. 321.
5. T. Hanna, *The Thought and Art of Albert Camus* (Chicago: Henry Regnery Co., 1958), p. 164.
6. A. Watts, *The Book* (New York: Pantheon Books, 1966), p. 90.
7. E. Kaelin, *An Existentialist Aesthetic* (Madison: The University of Wisconsin Press, 1966), p. 239.

8. D. Carr, in *Existential Philosophers: Kierkegaard to Merleau-Ponty*, edited by G. Schrader (New York: McGraw-Hill, 1967), p. 394.

9. *Ibid.*, p. 410.

10. W. Schutz, *Joy: Expanding Human Awareness* (New York: Grove Press, 1967), p. 29.

11. H. Furth, *Thinking Without Language: Psychological Implications of Deafness* (New York: Free Press, 1966), p. 198.

12. G. Hall, *Educational Problems*, Vol. 1 (New York: D. Appleton and Co., 1924), pp. 274-275.

13. M. Polanyi, *Personal Knowledge* (New York: Harper Torchbooks, Harper & Row, 1964), p. 78.

14. Middletown, Connecticut: Wesleyan University Press, 1964.

15. M. Richards, "Thoughts on Writing and Handcraft," *Craft Horizons*, XXVI (July/August 1966), 32-33, 41-43.

16. Watts, *op. cit.*, pp. 85-86.

17. P. Wheelwright, *Metaphor and Reality* (Bloomington: Indiana University Press, 1962), p. 57.

18. P. Koestenbaum, "Phenomenological Foundations for the Behavioral Sciences: The Nature of Facts," *Journal of Existentialism*, VI (Spring 1966), 315-316.

19. Polanyi, *op. cit.*, p. 81.

20. Koestenbaum, *op. cit.*, p. 319.

21. Watts, *op. cit.*, p. 61.

22. Koestenbaum, *op. cit.*, pp. 320-321.

23. L. Mumford, *The Conduct of Life* (New York: Harcourt, Brace, 1951), p. 35.

24. O. Barfield, in *The Importance of Language*, edited by M. Black (Englewood Cliffs: Prentice-Hall, Inc., 1962), pp. 51-71.

25. Cited in S. Langer, *Philosophy in a New Key* (New York: The New American Library, 1959), pp. 124-125.

26. Wheelwright, *op. cit.*, pp. 70-91.

27. *Ibid.*, pp. 72-73.

28. Kaelin, *op. cit.*, p. 248.

29. Wheelwright, *op. cit.*, p. 78.

30. I. Scheffler, *The Language of Education* (Springfield, Illinois: Charles C. Thomas, 1960), pp. 48-49.

31. Kaelin, *op. cit.*, p. 262.

32. Watts, *op. cit.*, p. 127.

33. M. McLuhan, *Understanding Media: The Extensions of Man* (New York: McGraw-Hill, 1965), p. 83.

34. *Ibid.*, p. 57.

35. J. Dewey, *Art as Experience* (New York: Minton, Balch and Co., 1934), p. 227.

36. "Concepts of Dance Therapy," *Group Psychotherapy*, Vol. XX (September-December 1967), 154-155.

37. McLuhan, *op. cit.*, p. 235.

38. "The Contribution of Dance to the Collective Unconscious," *Focus on Dance III*, edited by B. Wooten (Washington: American Association for Health, Physical Education, and Recreation, 1965), pp. 41-43.

39. Extensive literature concerning research on dance as communication may be obtained from the Center for Movement Research and Analysis, 8 East 12th Street, New York City.

40. Dewey, *op. cit.*, p. 106.

41. E. Gombrich, *Art and Illusion* (New York: Pantheon Books, 1956), p. 87.

42. V. Aldrich, "Visual Metaphor," *The Journal of Aesthetic Education*, II(January 1968), 73-86.

43. V. Aldrich, "Mothersill and Gombrich—The Language of Art," *The Journal of Philosophy*, LXII (1965), 573.

44. M. Mothersill, "Is Art a Language?" *Ibid.*, pp. 559-572.

45. *Ibid.*, p. 572. Whether or not visual metaphors can be asserted or denied is an epistemological question which is dealt with in the following chapter.

46. Dewey, *op. cit.*, p. 238.

47. D. Humphrey, *The Art of Making Dances* (New York: Holt, Rinehart and Winston, 1960), p. 104.

48. A. Watts, *Psychotherapy East and West* (New York: Pantheon Books, 1961), p. 193.

49. *Ibid.*

Chapter V

1. This chapter is a considerably expanded version of my article, "The Feeling/Notion Epistemological Paradigm," *Educational Theory*, Vol. 18 (Spring 1968), 125-132.

2. C. I. Lewis, *An Analysis of Knowledge and Valuation*, 1946. N. Malcolm, *Knowledge and Certainty*, 1963. B. Russell, *Human Knowledge*, 1948. A. Ayer, *The Problem of Knowledge*, 1956. J. Hintikka, *Knowledge and Belief*, 1962. A. Woozley, *Theory of Knowledge*, 1949. I. Scheffler, *Conditions of Knowledge*, 1965.

3. A. J. Ayer, *Language, Truth, and Logic* (New York: Dover Publications, [n.d.]), p. 112.

4. Scheffler, *op. cit.*, p. 107.

5. J. Dewey, *Psychology* (New York: Harper & Brothers, 1898), Chapters X through XVI.

6. M. Arnold, "The Status of Emotion in Contemporary Psychology," in *Present Day Psychology*, edited by A. Roback (New York: Philosophical Library, 1955), p. 170.

7. D. Arnstine, *Philosophy of Education* (New York: Harper & Row, 1967).

8. C. S. Peirce, *Values in a Universe of Chance*, edited by P. Wiener (New York: Doubleday Anchor Books, 1958), p. 130.

9. *Ibid.*, pp. 114 and 124.

10. Cited in C. Pailthorp, "Hintikka and Knowing that One Knows," *The Journal of Philosophy*, Vol. LXIV, No. 16 (August 24, 1967), 488.

11. A. Goldman, "A Causal Theory of Knowing," *The Journal of Philosophy*, Vol. LXIV, No. 12 (June 22, 1967), 372.

12. I. Thut, *The Story of Education: Philosophical and Historical Foundations* (New York: McGraw-Hill, 1957.).

13. Arnstine, *op. cit.*, pp. 3-6.

14. *Ibid.*, pp. 9-10.

15. *Ibid.*, pp. 188-193 contain specific statements regarding his conception of affectivity.

16. *Ibid.*, Chapter IX.

17. Creegan, "Recent Trends in the Psychology of Values," in Roback, *op. cit.*, p. 952.

18. N. Chiaromonte, "Albert Camus," *New Republic*, CXIV (April 29, 1946), 631.

19. A. Camus, *The Myth of Sisyphus* (New York: Vintage Books, Random House, 1959), pp. 3-48.

20. J.-P. Sartre, *Literary and Philosophical Essays* (New York: Collier Books, 1962), p. 40.

21. Camus, *op. cit.*, p. 14.

22. *Ibid.*, pp. 21ff.

23. W. Schutz, *Joy: Expanding Human Awareness* (New York: Grove Press, 1967), p. 74.

24. S. Langer, *Mind: An Essay on Human Feeling* (Baltimore: The Johns Hopkins Press, 1967).

25. M. McLuhan, *The Gutenberg Galaxy* (Toronto: University of Toronto Press, 1962), p. 26.

26. P. Wheelwright, *Metaphor and Reality* (Bloomington: Indiana University Press, 1962), p. 91.

27. Sartre, *op. cit.*, pp. 30-34.

28. F. Olafson, *Principles and Persons* (Baltimore: The Johns Hopkins Press, 1967), pp. 80-94.

29. Cited in S. Tenenbaum, "Implications of a Phenomenological Approach to Education," *Educational Theory*, XVII (October 1967), 345.

Chapter VI

1. New Haven, Conn.: Yale University Press, 1940.

2. Kurt Lewin, in the 1920's, also attempted to formulate a mathematical theory of behavior but failed on several grounds. His hodological geometry has been thoroughly discredited by mathematicians; his work was based not at all on empirical

premises; and, of greatest importance although his theory afforded much commentary on what a good theory should be, it never really came to grips with actual human behavior.

3. *Ibid.*, pp. 1-13.

4. M. Scharlemann, ed., *What, Then, Is Man?* (Saint Louis: Concordia Publishing House, 1958), pp. 79-81.

5. *Ibid.*, p. 81.

6. *Ibid.*, p. 79.

7. F. Kerlinger, *Foundations of Behavioral Research* (New York: Holt, Rinehart and Winston, 1964), pp. 10-12.

8. The paragraphs which follow on Nagel and Hempel are adapted from my paper, "Scientific Explanation of Literature," *Philosophy of Education*, edited by F. Villemain (Edwardsville: Southern Illinois University, 1966), pp. 112-118.

9. E. Nagel, *The Structure of Science; Problems in the Logic of Scientific Explanation* (New York: Harcourt, Brace and World, 1961), pp. 15-52. Since the paragraphs following are a summary of Nagel's treatment of explanation, specific footnotes are omitted.

10. *Ibid.*, pp. 51-52.

11. "The Function of General Laws in History," in *Theories of History*, ed. by P. Gardiner (Glencoe, Ill.: The Free Press, 1959), p. 1.

12. *Ibid.*, p. 5.

13. Berkeley and Los Angeles: University of California Press, 1966.

14. *Ibid.*, pp. 103-104.

15. *Ibid.*, p. 100.

16. B. Barry and B. Wolf, *Motives, Values, and Realities: A Framework for Counseling* (New York: Teachers College Press, 1965).

17. *Ibid.*, pp. 38-76.

18. E. Glanz, *Foundations and Principles of Guidance* (Boston: Allyn and Bacon, 1964), p. 98.

19. C. Rogers, *Client-Centered Therapy* (Boston: Houghton Mifflin Co., 1951), p. 481.

20. *Ibid.*, pp. 481-532.

21. "Two Divergent Trends," in *Existential Psychology*, edited by R. May (New York: Random House, 1961), pp. 85-93.

22. "Toward a Science of the Person," in *Behaviorism and Phenomenology*, edited by T. Wann (Chicago: The University of Chicago Press, 1964), pp. 109-133.

23. *Ibid.*, p. 119.

24. *Ibid.*, p. 121.

25. *Ibid.*, pp. 126-127.

26. Hull, *op. cit.*, p. 6.

27. A. Camus, *The Myth of Sisyphus* (New York: Vintage Books, Random House, 1959), p. 14.

Chapter VII

1. F. Molina, *Existentialism as Philosophy* (Englewood Cliffs, New Jersey: Prentice-Hall, Inc., 1962), pp. 1-3.
2. *Ibid.*, p. 4.
3. T. Hanna, *The Thought and Art of Albert Camus* (Chicago: Henry Regnery Co., 1958), p. xix.
4. This section is adapted from my article, by the same title, in the *International Review of Education*, Vol. XIV, No. 1, 1968, 97-102.
5. "What (if anything) to Expect from Today's Philosophers," *Time*, LXXXVII, January 7, 1966, 24-25.
6. New York: Philosophical Library.
7. *Existentialism in Education* (New York: Harper and Row, 1966).
8. D. Vandenberg: "Kneller, Heidegger and Death," *Educational Theory*, XV, July 1965, 217-221.
9. A. DeSoto: "Heidegger, Kneller, and Vandenberg," *Educational Theory*, XVI, July 1966, 239-241.
10. V. Morris: *Philosophy and the American School* (Boston: Houghton Mifflin, 1961), pp. 317, 383-400.
11. Morris, *op. cit.*, pp. 135-154.
12. C. Bowers: "Existentialism and Educational Theory," *Educational Theory* XV, (July 1965), 222-229.
13. L. Troutner: "What Can the Educator Learn from the Existential Philosopher?" *Philosophy of Education*, ed. by F. Villemain (Edwardsville: Southern Illinois Universty 1966), pp. 98-105.
14. Bowers, *op. ct.*, p. 223.
15. *Ibid.*, p. 227.
16. A Wirth: "Viktor E. Frankl and 'The Responsible Self'," *Educational Theory*, XII (October 1962), 241-246.
17. K. Winetrout: "Buber: Philosopher of the I-Thou Dialogue," *Educational Theory*, XIII (January 1963), 53-57.
18. D. Denton: "Albert Camus: Philosopher of Moral Concern," *Educational Theory*, XIV (April 1964), 99-102.
19. J. Willers: "Unamuno Centennial," *Educational Theory*, XV (October 1965), 317-320.
20. B. Hill: "Soren Kierkegaard and Educational Theory," *Educational Theory*, XVI (October 1966), 344-353.
21. *Philosophy and the American School, op. cit.*
22. *Ibid.*, pp. 87-88, 100-103.
23. *Ibid.*, pp. 204-207, 210-212.

24. *Ibid.*, pp. 304-308, 314-318.

25. J. D. Butler, *Four Philosophies and Their Practice In Education and Religion*, Third Edition (New York: Harper and Row, 1968), pp. 439-466.

26. P. G. Smith, *Philosophy of Education: Introductory Studies* (New York: Harper and Row, 1964, 1965), pp. 51-71.

Chapter VIII

1. R. Campbell and R. Gregg, eds., *Administrative Behavior In Education* (New York: Harper & Brothers, 1957), pp. 93-113.

2. B. Russell, *Authority and the Individual* (Boston: Beacon Press, 1960), pp. 74-75.

3. A. Camus, *Resistance, Rebellion, and Death* (New York: Alfred A. Knopf, 1961), p. 160.

4. A. Camus, *Caligula and Three Other Plays* (New York: Vintage Books, Random House, 1962), p. 227.

5. Princeton, N.J.: Van Nostrand, 1964.

6. T. Parsons and E. Shills, *Toward a General Theory of Action* (New York: Harper & Row, 1962), p. 190.

7. Efficiency and economy as models from industrial management and the criticism of this is the thesis of frequently cited, R. Callahan, *Education and the Cult of Efficiency* (Chicago: University of Chicago Press, 1962).

8. Parsons and Shills, *op. cit.*, pp. 193-194.

9. *Ibid.*, p. 194.

10. Russell, *op. cit.*, p. 51.

11. J. Lahr, "The Street Scene," *Evergreen Review*, Vol. 12 (October 1968), 90.

12. A. Camus, *The Rebel* (New York: Vintage Books, Random House, 1956), p. 276.

13. A. Camus, *The Myth of Sisyphus and Other Essays* (New York: Vintage Books, Random House, 1959), p. 105.

SUBJECT INDEX

Alienation, 4, 12-14, 123, 139-140

Educational Methodology, 5, 61, 98-100, 127-129, 135; examples of existential language in, 18-19, 57-59, 74-75, 77, 79-80

Educational Research, 5-10

Existential Language, defined, 79

Explanation, deductive, 105-107, 113-115; probabilistic, 107-108; historical, 108-109, 116; as-understanding, 117-120

Feelings, 61, 84, 87, 89-90, 93-97, 117

Fringe-Facts, 65-67; *contrast with precise-facts*, 148n

Genetic Theory of Language, 51-53

Gestures, 72-73

I-Sentences, 42, 119

Individuals, 20-21, 49-51

Isomorphisms-of-Experience, 53-55

Metaphors, 67-80, 144; body, 73-75; diaphor, 68-70; epi-phor, 68-69; musical, 73, 77-79; visual, 73, 75-77

Mr. 1948's, 144-145

Nootka Model of Language, 63

Ordinary Experience, defined, 17-19

Ordinary Language Analysis, 32-37, 57

Organizational Theory, 139-143

Perspectival Individuality, 49-50

Phenomenological Reduction, 14-15

Philosophy of Education, 5, 20-21, 125, 132-133

Plurisigns, defined, 64-66

Roles, 138-139

Social Laws, 9

Sociological-Nomothetic, 11-13, 20, 22-23, 59, 123

"Soul," 137-138, 144

Steno-Language, 37-38, 41-42, 103, 136-138, 143, 144-145; *see also precise-fact*, 148n

Successful Students, 145

Welterfahrendesleben, 8

NAME INDEX

159

Thut, I., 86, 152n
Tiryakian, E., 9
Troutner, L., 128-129

Unamuno, M., 129

Vandenberg, D., 126
Vargas, E., 142

Waismann, F., 39, 42
Watson, J., 7

Watts, A., 47-48, 49, 60, 63, 66, 71, 78-79
Wegener, P., 68
Wertheimer, M., 46
Wheelwright, P., 5, 37, 48, 49-50, 64-71, 76, 98, 148n
Whorf, B., 143
Winetrout, K., 129
Wirth, A., 129
Wittgenstein, L., 5, 26
Wolf, B., 111, 114
Woozley, A., 83